THE PRACTICE OF POETRY

BY THE SAME AUTHOR

Poetry

Patmos and Other Poems (1955)
Third Day Lucky (1958)
Two Ballads of the Muse (1960)
Begging the Dialect (1960)
The Dark Window (1962)
A Valedictory Poem (1963)
An Irish Gathering (1964)
A Ballad of Billy Barker (1965)
Inscriptions (1967)
Because of This (1968)
The Hold of Our Hands (1968)
Selected Poems 1947-1967 (1968)
An Irish Album (1969)
Georges Zuk: Selected Verse (1969)
Answers (1969)
The Hunting Dark (1971)
Two Hundred Poems from the Greek Anthology (1971)

Criticism

John Ruskin: The Final Years (1955)
The Poetic Pattern (1956)
Cavalier Poets (1960)
Poetry (1963)
The Writings of J. M. Synge (1971)

Editions

J. M. Synge: Translations (1961)
J. M. Synge: Four Plays and the Aran Islands (1962)
J. M. Synge: Collected Poems (1962)
Edward Thomas: Selected Poems (1962)
Selected Poems of Byron (1965)
David Gascoyne: Collected Poems (1965)
J. M. Synge: Riders to the Sea (1969)
David Gascoyne: Collected Verse Translations (with Alan Clodd) (1970)
Synge/Petrarch (1971)

Anthologies

Viewpoint: An Anthology of Poetry (1962)
Six Irish Poets (1962)
Poetry of the Thirties (1964)
Five Poets of the Pacific Northwest (1964)
Poetry of the Forties (1968)
The Cavalier Poets (1970)

Symposia

The World of W. B. Yeats (with Ann Saddlemyer) (1965)
Irish Renaissance (with David R. Clark) (1965)
Herbert Read: A Memorial Symposium (1970)

THE PRACTICE OF POETRY

by

Robin Skelton

HEINEMANN

LONDON

Heinemann Educational Books Ltd

LONDON EDINBURGH MELBOURNE TORONTO

SINGAPORE JOHANNESBURG NEW DELHI

AUCKLAND IBADAN HONG KONG

NAIROBI

ISBN 0 435 18817 8
ISBN 0 435 18818 6 (paperback edition)

Published by
Heinemann Educational Books Ltd
48 Charles Street, London W1X 8AH
Made and printed in Great Britain by
William Clowes and Sons, Limited
London, Beccles and Colchester

Contents

Acknowledgements

The author and publishers thank the undermentioned for the following poems or extracts: for the poems by Robin Skelton, McClelland & Stewart, Oxford University Press, Routledge & Kegan Paul; for 'Nantucket', William Carlos Williams and New Directions; for 'Hunting Song' from *The Sky Clears, Poetry of the American Indians*, William Carlos Williams and the University of Nebraska Press; for the 'Mahi Lament' from *African Poetry*, Ulli Beier and Cambridge University Press; for 'Who's in the Next Room?', the Trustees of the Hardy Estate and Macmillan Ltd; for 'An Epitaph', the Literary Trustees of Walter de la Mare, and The Society of Authors as their representatives; for 'Worksheets', Thomas Kinsella and The Dolman Press Ltd; for 'Soft Toy', Thomas Kinsella; for 'Considering Junk', Tony Connor and Oxford University Press; for 'The Song of the Mad Prince', the Literary Trustees of Walter de la Mare and The Society of Authors as their representative; for 'Housing Development', H. R. Hays and the Kayak Press, San Francisco; for 'Poem of the Fancy', John Knight and the Cresset Press; for 'Invocation', Kathleen Raine and Hamish Hamilton Ltd; for 'Missing Dates', William Empson and Chatto & Windus Ltd; for 'Paradise Lost', Gordon Wharton and The University of Reading Press; for 'Do Not Go Gentle into That Good Night', the Trustees of the late Dylan Thomas and J. M. Dent & Son Ltd; for a poem from 'The Seven Last Poems from the Memoirs of Uncle Harry', Tony Connor and the Yorick Press; for 'The Voice of Authority', Kingsley Amis; for 'Have a Good Time', W. H. Auden and Faber & Faber Ltd; for 'Monologue d'outre Tombe' and 'Haiku', Babbette Deutch and Curtis Brown; for 'Acquainted with one Night' from *The Poetry of Robert Frost*, Edward Connery Lathan and the Estate of Robert Frost; for 'Where Knock is Open Wide' and 'The Shape of Fire' from *Collected Poems of Theodore Roethke*, and 'Yesterday all the past. The language of size' from *Collected Shorter Poems 1930–1944* by W. H. Auden; for 'Choruses from The Rock' from *Collected Poems 1909–1962* by T. S. Eliot, and extracts from Canto XXXVI and Canto LXXXI from *The Cantos of Ezra Pound*, Faber & Faber Ltd; for 'A Ballade of Suicide' from *Collected Poems of G. K. Chesterton*, Miss Collins and Methuen & Son Ltd; extract from 'A Refusal to Mourn', the Trustees of the Late Dylan Thomas and J. M. Dent & Sons Ltd; for 'The House on the Hill', Edward Arlington Robinson, Macmillan & Co. Ltd; for extract from 'The Green Shepherd' copyright 1956 by Louis Simpson, Reprinted from *A Dream of Governors*, Louis Simpson, by permission of Wesleyan University Press, first published in *The New Yorker*; extract from 'The Odyssey' translated by E. V. Rieu, Penguin Books Ltd; for 'A Present', Daryl Hine and Atheneum Publishers; for 'Jimmie's got a girl' e e cummings and MacGibbon & Kee Ltd; for 'It was twenty years ago I saw the fox', Phoebe Hesketh and Rupert Hart-Davis; for the West African children's song, the magazine *Black Orpheus*. The publishers have not been able to trace the sources of quotations in all cases and will be happy to hear from any unacknowledged copyright holders.

Preface

This is the third book I have written about the making of poetry. In the first, *The Poetic Pattern* (Routledge & Kegan Paul, 1956), I attempted to explore the nature of the poetic process and to come to some general conclusions about the function and value of poetry. In the second, *Poetry* (English Universities Press, 1962), which was published in the *Teach Yourself* series, I tried to explain simply how to read poetry with appreciation and then suggested a number of ways in which one might begin to write it. Since 1962 I have taught the writing of poetry at the University of Victoria and have developed a number of new approaches to the problem. During these years I have searched unsuccessfully for a book that combines technical instruction in verse craftsmanship with instruction in the manipulation of the imagination and the development of individual poetic vision. I have therefore attempted to fill the gap with a book that I hope may prove of use both to young poets and to teachers of writing.

It is not a comprehensive book. It is, perhaps, only a preliminary sketch for much work which remains to be done, and if I were to give it a sub-title it might well read "Notes towards the Creation of a new Gradus ad Parnassum". In making it I have been greatly assisted by many people, and especially by my students who have performed the oddest experiments with patience and good humour and who have allowed me to quote their work. I have not attached names to their individual poems and near-poems as I believe that several of them will become known as poets and might find this book an embarrassment in years to come. I would, however, like to mention here the names of those who have contributed most to the making of this book. These are Maeford Slocombe, Heather Boucher, John Harding, Susan Vaulkhard, F. C. Pye, Elizabeth Webber, Alan Jones, David Bentley, Brian Dedora, Denis Beames, and G. M. Seeds. I am grateful to these, and to countless others over the years since 1952 when I first began my experiments, for helping me in my explorations and for teaching me so much.

The University of Victoria,   R.S.
British Columbia.

ONE Finding the Word Hoard

A poem is an exploration rather than a disquisition. It is not a way of stating effectively an already known idea or message. It is a way of struggling with the excitements and tensions of the words surrounding and embodying one's attitude towards a particular subject until those excitements and tensions result in the creation of a pattern and at least a temporary conviction of having achieved some kind of resolution. Though Pope may have told us that

> True Wit is Nature to Advantage dressed,
> What oft was thought but ne'er so well expressed,
> *Essay on Criticism*

he understood as well as any man that a thought is transfigured by its expression, and that a feeling may not be even vaguely intelligible until it is expressed in words. Tony Connor once said, as his recipe for writing a poem: 'Invent a jungle and then explore it'. Our problem is finding out how to invent that jungle, how to detect the verbal excitements surrounding our perceptions, and how to discover in ourselves a confusion rich enough to compel us to investigate it.

We often know where the densest jungles are to be found. We are aware of our points of greatest sensitivity, and can recognize some of our emotional problems. Knowing that one has a complex, confused, and emotionally stimulating attitude towards ships or shoes or sealing wax, however, is not enough. It is not enough partly because the very attaching of those simple labels makes these subjects seem in themselves simple, and partly because if we explore further we may well find that ships and shoes and sealing wax are merely defensive euphemisms for an obsession with drowning, a nervous tension at the thought of travelling, and a very disturbed attitude towards authority and law. But, even if we, or our psychiatrist, or our teacher, discover this, we are still possessed only of a few words in our hoard and we may not be very excited about them.

We have to be excited by language itself, by its wayward richness, as well as by ideas and images. The language of poetry is the language of excitement; excitement generates it and it generates excitement. In order to discover exactly what subject matter and what language one has to start off with, one can perform a number of manœuvres. One manœuvre is to set down, on loose sheets of paper, every night before retiring, every word that comes into one's head over a period of around twenty minutes. This should be done every night for a minimum of ten and a maximum of fourteen nights. The pages must not be read over after they have been written, or looked at at all until the ten- or fourteen-night period is over. Then, surveying this confusion of diary jottings, random speculations, word games, nonsense, obscenity, facetiousness, and boredom, one usually discovers something interesting. Around the fourth or fifth day obsessive themes occur; sometimes lines of verse occur; most often, however, one discovers that one has been deeply concerned over something that one had not ever guessed to be at all important. I say one *discovers* this, but in fact, of course, what one discovers may be far from the truth; it may itself be an evasion or a disguise. It is, however, quite certainly a jungle that is going to be worth exploring. This exercise is not entirely a subject-hunt, however. It also is a deliberate exercise in what I would like to call non-writing. One has not been writing for an audience; one has not been composing a journal, or scribbling a letter; one has only been letting one's mind range around at random to see what it may turn up. Because this is non-writing it is free writing. One should never, at least as a beginner, start off a piece of writing by saying 'I am going to make a poem'. The magnitude of the task, and the arrogance of attempting it, get in the way of easy thought and easy associational flow. One should simply say 'I am playing with words' or 'I am doodling in words' or 'I wonder what happens if I start off by saying . . . '

Non-writing enables one to knock the language around a bit. Syntax is marred or non-existent. Language is looser and freer. And words, when one is tired (remember that this is done just before retiring), often come in odd groups and achieve strange juxtapositions.

Language itself is a route to perception. One must learn to give language freedom, to release it to perform. Later one may decide to treat it more rigorously, but at the beginning of a poem, a piece of non-writing, or even a poetic career, one must give it its head. For one thing, the language of excitement can derive from the excitement of language. And if one can make oneself associate words freely, without worrying too much about meanings, the words themselves will produce meanings enough.

There is another exercise which is both entertaining and valuable, but it requires five or six people to do it. The leader of the group secretes in his pocket or her purse three small objects. It doesn't really matter what they are, though it is best for them to be immediately recognizable and commonplace enough to have played some part in every person's ordinary experience. The leader, stopwatch in hand, lifts up the first object, and this is the visual signal for all the others to write down as many words as they possibly can in two minutes. The first word need have nothing to do with the object. The object is only a visual starting pistol for the race. After the two minutes are over the words should be counted. Scores vary enormously. Some people associate freely from the very beginning and register a score somewhere in the fifties. Some get blocked by trying to make sense of what they are writing, by finding themselves wanting to put down a taboo word, or by simply getting stuck on one word and being unable to think of any other word at all. It should be pointed out now that words can be repeated, that obscenity doesn't matter, and that speed is the thing. The second object is then shown, and, after a break for flexing the writing fingers, the third. Most people increase their score over the three objects, but not all. Some increase from A to B and then reduce the count for C. Some people only block at the last object. But whatever the score is, the result is that the people concerned have not had time to think about the words; they have simply associated them with one another. Unselfconscious verbal free-association is characteristic of the writing of much poetry.

This exercise makes it easy to see and demonstrate the variety of verbal associations. There is association by contrast; *White* may follow *Black*. There is association by sound, as in *Sing, Thing, Thin, Bin*. There are associations deriving from established patterns of experience. Some of these patterns may be generally available, such as following *Grass* with *Green*, or *Judge* with *Wig*. Some may be entirely private. I myself associate *Sea* with *Stone* because of my childhood experience of the East Yorkshire coast. Some associations are punning. *Red* may be followed by *Book*. Sometimes the associations form clumps rather than sequences. Thus *Fly* may be followed by *Spider*, but also by *Aeroplane* or *Cunning*; the different meanings of the word *Fly* have all crowded in upon the racing mind. There is also rhythmic association. *Hinder* may be followed by *Broken* or *Lovely*, simply because all these words are composed of an accented syllable followed by an unaccented one. A tune often emerges.

A typical list is the following made by one of my students. I have arranged it so as to indicate the simple rhythmical groupings.

> Battery Juice Red Gold
> Oh Blue Silver Black
> Empty Star Hot Cold
> Ice Bear Fur Fire
> Stove Rug Cat Tail
> There Now Up Trees
> No Down Earth Ground
> Wet Leaf Vein Brittle
> Hand Sand
> Water Sun
> Cloud Gun
> Black Who?

There are rhyming elements here, and towards the end, the hint of a narrative. The simple rhythm breaks on the word *brittle* and then reasserts itself.

You will observe that this free-association game leads one to use, unselfconsciously, many of the devices of poetry and verse. One begins to understand that when the poet produces a surprising phrase it is frequently because he has made a quick associative leap, one so quick that in all probability he cannot himself say what has happened until he has looked over his work. I'd be prepared to swear that when Shakespeare wrote 'Pity like a naked new-born babe striding the blast', he wrote it quickly and without conscious thought. *Pity like a* was the first verbal unit. With *pity* one associates the objects of pity. One of these is nakedness. Helplessness is added by *new-born babe*. Association by contrast, a reaching out instinctively for dramatic surprise, gives us one of the actions which a baby just cannot do. It cannot stride. It can't, being new-born, even crawl. And therefore *striding* emerges onto the page. From the smallness of the child to the vastness of the heavens and the wind is another association by contrast, but the word *blast* also has associations with the infliction of suffering and therefore links with the word *Pity* which began the whole poetic movement.

This is necessarily hypothesis, but my example does, I think, illustrate the importance of learning to make and to trust associative leaps.

It may also suggest, by its rhythmic quality, just how rhythmic language itself tends to assist the associative process. Many poets have said that if they begin to write in a given metre, or to a given tune, after a while the words begin to come of themselves, and astonish with their imaginative qualities, their surprising associative leaps. Louis MacNeice has gone on record as saying this, and so has G. S. Fraser.

Of course, excitement does not only derive from associative leaps. When we are emotionally disturbed we use language, we say, figuratively. When, in anger, we call a man a *filthy bastard*, we do not in fact mean that he is illegitimate or physically dirty; we mean to suggest that he has qualities which we associate with illegitimacy and uncleanliness. The word *filthy* is used to mean lacking in any kind of spiritual purity, and we have at the back of our minds the notion that it is possible to describe spiritual conditions by comparing them to colours. His bastardy is intended to suggest an unfortunate family background, a lack of good breeding (we are comparing the human creature to the domestically bred animal here), and therefore a lack of a proper system of values. In making all these associations we are, of course, revealing social prejudice. When we say 'That was a lousy thing to do' we are implying that, as cleanliness may be next to godliness, so being louse-ridden must be an ungodly condition.

These are commonplaces of vituperation. More inventive people use more elaborate language. If a man is called, as he might well be called in a Jacobean or Elizabethan play, an *addle-pated varlet* a slightly more complex series of messages is being created. His low social condition is indicated by *varlet* and this low social condition is taken to imply lack (again) of good breeding and also of intelligence, imagination, self-respect, and character. He is fit for nothing but to be a servant. He is *addle-pated* because his brains (in his pate, which is egg-shaped) are of no use. An addled egg is useless, and odoriferous, and the product of carelessness on the part of a housewife, or laziness on the part of a hen that has not seen fit to finish the job and hatch out the chick; it is indicative simultaneously of a birth lost and a meal spoiled. It is waste matter to be thrown away, and it is physically offensive to all who come near it.

This figurative language is obviously characterized by its use of multiple associations. Each word has many meanings, as do words in poetry. We must recognize, however, that, because we use figurative language when we are emotionally disturbed, when we read figurative language we interpret it as revealing emotional disturbance. *Wild and whirling words* are thought to indicate mental and emotional unbalance.

How can we learn to give language this figurative and multiple-meaning quality, without, of course, making use of clichés and commonplaces whose emotional effectiveness has been reduced by familiarity ?

One way is to indulge in nonsense. Nonsense is difficult to write, for the average reader is so used to believing that all verbal messages contain meaning that when he sees one, especially if its shape is like that of other and immediately intelligible verbal messages, he supposes it to have meaning. Consider the difference, however, between reading *Flackzz Bronp Flink* and *Flackzz Bronp Flinkly*. In the first version we tend to assume that it is, if language at all, a foreign one. In the second version we think we are beginning to get a message for the *ly* ending suggests an adverb. Thus we read the statement as if it were *Flackzz* (name of thing), *Bronp* (verb), *Flinkly* (adverb). If we go further and add enough to the nonsense to make a syntactical shape even more recognizable then we have a more intense illusion of meaningful statement. Thus *The Flackzz was Bronp Flinkly* almost appears to make sense.

This may seem a digression from our main concern, which is with giving language emotional intensity and enabling us to be surprised by perceptions which language itself provides when we indulge in verbal play. It is not, however, a digression, for it leads on to the playing of an entertaining game invented by the French Surrealists. This is a form of verbal Consequences and it reveals just to what extent syntax can create meaning, and nonsense can imply emotion.

We need a minimum of five players for the game. Each has a sheet of paper which he conceals from the sight of his neighbour. A writes the definite article and an adjective (*The green*). B writes a noun in the singular (*elephant*). C writes a verb in the third person singular which takes an object (*rattles*). D writes the definite article and an adjective (*the truthful*). E ends the sentence with a noun in the singular or plural (*magistrate*). We now have the statement 'The green elephant rattles the truthful magistrate.' It may not be a wise or profound statement, but because it is a syntactical one we accept it as a message, and as a statement of some kind of truth. Now, the kind of truth involved here is obviously that of dream, or nightmare, or the *wild and whirling words* of poetry. If we make our syntactical shape a different, and slightly more complex one, we get even stranger results. The conditional sentence is almost always productive of strangeness. One result of breaking up a conditional sentence in this way might be: (*If the yellow*) (*alarm clock*) (*eats*) (*the noisy*) (*mountain*), (*then the disastrous*) (*hornpipe*) (*knows*) (*the golden*) (*sandwich*). We find ourselves, here, believing in the truth of the statement, at least momentarily, for if our premise is an impossibility then it is not illogical for its consequence to be an impossibility also. This type of game is played in much poetry. Consider, for example, the lines:

> She walks in beauty, like the night
> Of cloudless climes and starry skies;
> And all that's best of dark and bright
> Meet in her aspect and her eyes . . .
> > Byron

Now, we might not swallow the magnificent statement that *all that's best of dark and bright meet in her aspect and her eyes*, if we had not already agreed to accept her walking *in beauty like the night*. We accepted this because the word *like* made us feel that there must be grounds for comparison; we accepted that such grounds must exist because the syntax depended upon such grounds existing. Thus the poet has given us a credible statement *(she walks in beauty,)* forced an irrational image upon us by introducing it with a pseudo-scientific or objective *like*, and then made us accept a wild generalization with practically no definable meaning at all.

We accept this material, however, not merely because syntax has convinced us, but because improbability and extremeness of expression made us intuit the presence of emotion. We recognize an emotional truth largely because it is the only truth available for us to recognize.

It is a sad fact that sensible, level-headed poetry rarely moves us. Thus if we wish to describe the beauty of a woman, and, more importantly, to convince others that we are in love with her, we should not say:

> My love is delicate as a rose,
> That's newly sprung in June:
> Her voice is like the melodie
> That's sweetly played in tune.

We should throw away all those rational appeals to observation and adducable evidence and say:

> O, my Luve's like a red red rose
> That's newly sprung in June:
> O, my Luve's like the melodie
> That's sweetly played in tune.

Though here, still, we indicate comparisons we are not specific about

7

them. Because we are not specific as to the precise associations of Rose and Tune that we want to use, all the associations come crowding in. Another technique is to avoid simile altogether, and to use metaphor. We do not compare, we transform. This process can be illustrated by an imaginary dialogue.

A: I feel that the passage of time constantly reminds us of how we grow old. It is like a mirror in which we see our features altering.

B: Why not transform it into a mirror, then you can look in it?

A: If I look in it I see that my features wither like flowers do.

B: Why don't you transform your features into a flower? Then you can see what happens.

A: If I am a withered flower I am thrown out on the rubbish dump among all the grass cuttings and rotten fall-apples.

B: Hold it! Aren't there other fruit than fallen apples? After all, apples suggest Eden, the fall of man, sexual temptation, and that's another subject entirely. You're a woman. What sort of complexion have you got?

A: Well, its been called a peach complexion. Girls are often called peaches.

B: Great! Now, if you are thrown out with the rotten peaches, what time of year is it?

A: Autumn, of course. The end of the summer. The beginning of winter.

B: Then why don't you deal with it that way?

A: All right . . . er . . .

> All things that pass
> Are woman's looking glass;
> They show her how her bloom must fade,
> And she herself be laid
> With withered roses in the shade;
> With withered roses and the fallen peach,
> Unlovely, out of reach
> Of summer joy that was.

Christina Rossetti, in all probability, did not get the first verse of her *Passing and Glassing* by means of this kind of internal argument, but she might well have done. A valuable exercise is to conduct such internal arguments, beginning with a cliché or obvious simile and seeing where it can lead. We might, rather frivolously, start off one such dialogue thus:

A: You know, Professor X has a face just like a fish!

B: Turn him into one.

A: What sort of fish?

B: Well, he's a bit sluggish. A lazy fish. And he's very devious and a bit ruthless. A pike.

A: Fine. But if he's a fish how does he live? What are his characteristics?

B: He lives in gloom at the bottom of a river. Use 'subaqueous'— it sounds a bit professorial and pedantic, somehow. And he has savage teeth, and lurks in wait. Come to think of it, that academic gown is sort of watery and flowing.

A: Ah! Slily in subaqueous gloom,
　　　the folding robes of water
　　　　stirring to his . . .
　　to his what?

B: Well, he's a Maths Professor, isn't he?

A: . . . stirring to his calculation
　　er . . . stirring as he calculates
　　　　his theorem of slaughter.

B: Do you calculate a theorem?

A: I don't think so. You can't say Calculus though—too clicking and rattly. Why not 'formulates': that sounds pedantic too.

B: He can't formulate a theorem, can he? I mean, I thought Euclid had done all that already.

A: . . . formulates
　　hypotheses of slaughter,

B: Ahh!

A: He is the father of the stream, . . . er . . . the darkness of the stream, the lurking death, the . . .

B: Great! You don't need me any more. I'll go now.

A: Slily in subaqueous gloom,
　　　the folding robes of water

  stirring as he formulates
  hypotheses of slaughter,

  he is the darkness of the stream,
  the lurking death, the cunning
  intellect of human greed
  that mocks the rivers running.

  B: Just popped back to say it's terrible but at least it's got away from being a silly poem about old fishface. Seems to be about some kind of warmonger, wouldn't you say ? Funny how things develop.

 It is giving oneself the freedom, even perhaps the irresponsibility, to let things develop, that matters. The poem one *means* to write doesn't matter. The poem that matters is the one that gets itself written.

This is a constant source of difficulty to many poets, both beginners and others. One means to write about one subject, but the poem insists on tackling another one. One really means to describe, let us say, a city street in San Francisco, but the Eiffel Tower will insist on being present. Sometimes one finds that what started off as a fairly respectable poem about being in love turns into a poem of such sexual explicitness that one is embarrassed.

This last problem is one of the most difficult for the young poet to cope with. I have known young poets become so disturbed at the supposed self-revelations in their poetry that they have become unable to face writing at all, much less showing their work to others. This is, I explain to them, the result of their failing to understand exactly what has happened. In writing a poem one not only exaggerates emotions for the sake of the poem, one also allows the language of the poem to develop a direction and purpose of its own. Thus the result is a poem which is always a distorted version of one's real feelings, and may well even be almost complete fiction. One has thrown away all the doubts, hesitancies, and absurdities that attend one's emotional experiences and kept (and exaggerated) only the attitudes useful to the poem. If the poem is a good one, one reads it over and is convinced by it. One says ' My God, do I really feel like that ?' And the good poem says earnestly, 'Yes, of course you do. It must come from your deepest self for, if you recall, half of these words appear to occur instinctively. You were inspired, my friend. This is the real you!' Then the writer says, 'Well, I suppose I do feel like that!' and goes out and finds a psychiatrist, or his best friend, or gets drunk.

Poems have to be persuasive, after all. One should, however, be careful not to be brainwashed by one's own poetry. The Muse is a practical joker, and one has to be careful about those inspirations. She provides us with universal truths about different aspects of human nature and human experience; she transforms us, temporarily into representative men and women. If she has a mind to, she will make a pacifist write a poem betraying savage and vindictive feelings, and she will cause the atheist to write mystical verse. The contentious, argumentative Landor wrote some of the most plaintively delicate and graceful poems in the language, and the number of gentle, kindly, withdrawn people who have written battle hymns is countless. A man's poems do not constitute his self-portrait or his autobiography; they constitute his discoveries.

No matter how often one says these things, however, it is always perfectly clear that somehow one's poems are deeply true of oneself and one's hidden character. Young poets do not easily develop that humility which believes that the poem is more important than the poet, and that a reputation for lechery, or alcoholism, or some other depravity, is a reasonable price to pay for the completion of a work of art, however false that reputation may be.

How can we make it clear, to ourselves or to others, that the business of making poetry, of making passionate statements, need not lead to self-betrayal ? There is one exercise which does this job pretty well, and also reveals and teaches something else about poetry. This is the verbal collage.

A collage, in art, is made up of scraps and fragments taken from other places and pasted together to form a new whole. Verbal collages are similarly composed. It is easy, of course, to make funny ones from fragments of the daily newspaper or women's magazines. It is so easy that it is hardly worth doing. It is more entertaining, and difficult, to try for a serious collage. One can choose to do these by restricting one's source material, to let us say, a small number of authors, or even the published letters of one particular author, or one can simply trust in serendipity and pick one's fragments from anything whatsoever. As an illustration of verbal collages here are some taken from the work of my students.

Collage from Byron's Letters

The women here give me no rest,
But if they get me a name,
And at least some admiration, which is food and drink—
there is no need for further explanation.
I hold virtue to be a feeling, not a principle.

My own friends consider me a divine subject for
    example and reproof
What a curse I have been to you and everyone
Hunted, pestered and bored to death by fledgling poets,
But I don't regret the ill my scribbling may have done.

My movements are as uncertain as my temperament
And what I am doing now is of not much consequence—
Falling in love twenty times a month
And I am to be married at last—
Which will have the charm of novelty to recommend it.

It is now too late to commence the innocence of youth
Yet my health and intellect won't allow me to dissipate.
I am damned and dunned, by collectors and Christians
    alike;
But the women here—they are all beautiful.

        Collage: The Selected Letters of Henry James
It's mortally slow and stupid here,
A thrilling atmosphere.
In the uneasy gloom shines an angel,
Often sad and bitter, but never dull. Once,
You were in exile,
And now you carry a classic wound,
A man of the past, of a dead generation.
Was such a pitch of virtue ever before attained?

At the thought of a study of this kind
My eyes fill with heavenly tears,
My heart throbs with a divine courage,
A lone survivor at the bottom of an abyss
My silences are hideous, and history repeats itself;
I'm on the sofa, with my hair down, slowly and serenely
Dying—A thing to go barefoot to see.
Thank heaven there is another art.

        Collage from Multiple Sources

HEADLINE—POLICE DUCK BOMBS IN DUBLIN

'We will do nothing unless we are forced.'

All I have seen of this world are back doors and kitchens.
As a child I took to swallowing nickels,

Lurking about the Griffith Park Observatory,
Joy riding in a milk truck,
Ratting my hair . . . with a real rat.

'We will do nothing unless we are . . .'

Click click click
Photographs and graphs
Questions questions questions . . .
The Principle of Equal Sacredness

'Who are you ?'
The twin brother of a hypocrite brick wall,
A sentimentalist behind a Southern Comfort image,
A suicidal fussbudget . . .
No, I'm John Lennon.

'His background is relatively normal
American Bourgeoisie,
The second son of a dentist
From Washington, D.C.'
(As if it were a whole new thing to ponder.)

'We will do nothing unless . . . '

'Where did you come from ?'
I did not like the way you cut up the east,
Sandwiched between electricity and eccentricity,
So . . . a frangipani flower over one ear,
I made the leap
   (I was driving a bulldozer at the time)
      from Pre-History
         to the Twentieth Century!

'We will do nothing.'

Mother,
Supermen are hard to find.
The older you get the more it costs you . . .
Throwing up the past,
I dream of impotence and death.
Jumping is still the city's favourite method,
But there are no high buildings here.
Just freedom.
Isolated from the world, high on a hill
Among the flowers, the gardens . . . a penal paradise.

Read on Mother . . .
Try to forget you are a packrat like me,
Try to break the sleazy squirrel habit.

Cheer up Mother . . .
An umbrella is a status symbol in New Guinea,
Wiltwyck is *not* just an 'ordinary' prison.

These are, of course, some of the more interesting ones I have had brought to me. Because they are interesting, however, they make the point. The act of making a poem is as much an act of arrangement and selection as of invention and original imagination and one can make disturbing poetry of attitudes and beliefs that are not one's own. One can indeed, make poetry from material that appears, at first blush, to be distinctly non-poetic.

My students tell me that making collages like this is a tremendous relief from the pressure of personal investigation attendant upon trying to learn to write poetry. They also tell me that, by making poems in this way, they find their sense of the possibilities of the medium greatly enlarged. After all, they have pointed out, one can make a poem by doing a collage of one's own notebook material—patchworking it together. This is an excellent thing to do for poems do not always occur as a series of connected perceptions in a proper sequence. Some poems occur as random fragments over a long period. It is as well to make verbal collages as often as possible. It trains, too, the conscious awareness of the writer, and makes it easier for him to revise and polish his own work.

In this chapter I have concerned myself largely with limbering-up exercises. I have talked about the importance of learning to associate freely, to play verbal games that result in odd and emotionally disturbing word combinations, to develop a habit of taking a metaphor and riding it as far as it will go, and to learn to select and rearrange already existing material. These limbering-up exercises may not result in poems. Frequently they will result in total frustration. They will, however, lead to a recognition that behind the profundities of poetry lie a number of highly irresponsible attitudes towards language. Language is to be knocked about, played with, mistreated, and twisted: it is not to be our master, but our servant, and if it really becomes our servant it will lead us to perceptions and visions we never thought we could achieve.

It is not enough, however, to learn to dream constructively, associate freely, and enjoy surprising oddities of expression. We must learn to order, to arrange, and to choose the right voice for the right poem. Poetry begins in freedom, but moves onward through discipline.

TWO Arranging the Word Hoard

The writing of poetry is as much a matter of arranging verbal excitements as of discovering them. Moreover the arrangement must be such that every word has a function in the whole, and no word can be omitted. Learning to arrange words involves learning to think easily and freely in a particular fashion. The writer who is too conscious of the act of arranging his words is one who will find it difficult to make those associative leaps which are essential if he is to write powerfully and vividly, for he will be constantly pausing to check on the shapes he is making.

The act of arrangement is also the act of selection. One must choose only the most significant ideas and images for one's poem. Too much detail is distracting and makes the poem move sluggishly. It is often helpful to begin with a situation where an emotionally significant selection has already been made.

When we think back to our earliest memories we do not, usually, recall every detail of our experience. Many of these seem to be details of no real importance, and yet they insist on being recalled at the expense of, we suppose, much more important facts. Thus, we find ourselves with a series of only vaguely related fragments of experience, and these fragments carry for each of us a significance entirely disproportionate to their superficial content. I have found it useful to suggest to students that they make a list of ten or twelve images that occur to them on thinking back to their earliest childhood and arrange them in what seems a pleasing order. They are not to connect them up into sentences, or explain them. The words and phrases are to be those which present the actual sensations involved, uninterpreted and unadorned with hindsight. A typical image list of this kind is:

> Brown wood.
> Sharp corners.
> Head bump.
> Soft carpet.

>Warm.
>Very still.
>Big shoes.

This is not poetry, or even embryonic poetry. It would not even begin to be intelligible if one did not know it referred to a childhood memory. Even if one knows this, however, the message conveyed is elliptical. It is a memory of a small child standing under a table, very still, aware of the sharp corners on the horizontal bars of the gate-leg, and feeling warm and secure, the carpet soft under his bare feet, seeing the legs and huge shoes of his father pass by. It is one of my own memories. My students' image lists are not so easy for me to interpret. I do not always ask them what their lists refer to; their messages are not important. I am only concerned that they should struggle with the problem of presenting the essence of an experience.

The list above is as it occurred to me, and not yet arranged. A simple arrangement would result in:

>Soft warm carpet.
>Brown wood.
>Sharp corners.
>Head Bump.
>Very still.
>Big shoes.

We can now, if we wish, turn it all into simple sentences, thus:

>The carpet is soft, warm.
>The brown wood
>has sharp corners.
>My head bumps.
>I am very still.
>He has big shoes.

This kind of list is, of course, hardly poetry, but it is not dissimilar to some primitive poetry and to some poetry of the twentieth century. An elliptical presentation of the childhood viewpoint occurs, for example, in Theodore Roethke's dramatic monologue, *Where Knock is Open Wide*. The first few lines run:

>A kitten can
>Bite with his feet;
>Papa and Mamma
>Have more teeth.

> Sit and play
> Under the rocker
> Until the cows
> All have puppies

This records thoughts and interpretations as well as images. William Carlos Williams provides us with another example of an image list in *Nantucket*.

> Flowers through the window
> lavender and yellow
>
> changed by white curtains—
> Smell of cleanliness—
>
> Sunshine of late afternoon—
> On the glass tray
>
> a glass pitcher, the tumbler
> turned down, by which
>
> a key is lying—And the
> immaculate white bed

Here the poet has done no more than paint a picture, but the picture is beautifully ordered. There is light here. The light is suggested first by *the window*, is given colour by *lavender and yellow*, and intensified by *white curtains*. It is reinforced by the impression of *cleanliness* which, though it is recorded as a *smell*, gives us a general visual impression also, and is emphasized again by *Sunshine*. The translucencies of *glass* are presented to us three times, by the *tray*, the *pitcher*, and the *tumbler*, and whiteness recurs when we look at the *bed*. The *key* may or may not be shining; in the middle of all this light we must feel, however, that it is positively radiant. What does the poem mean? It means that the poet has wished to record, to recreate, a picture because he likes it. In so doing, he has given us a vision of radiance, cleanliness, and order that is in itself almost a religious message.

One cannot hope to succeed as well as William Carlos Williams in one's first attempts. One can, however, emulate him in moving on from making an image-list from childhood, to making an image-list from the present. This is more difficult because the selection has to be done by oneself; it is not made by the defects of recollection. It is interesting to suggest that a whole group of people make an image-list from their impressions of a scene they all know well. The differences in selection reveal clearly just how each writer finds himself picking details that either support a particular emotional attitude towards the scene or enable him to make his pattern stimulating. Two image-lists of the same scene, for example, run:

(i)	White Stone.	(ii)	Huge wall.
	Carved forms.		Swinging glass.
	Empty Glass		Low voices.
	Small walkers.		Book smell.

These describe the University of Victoria Library. The first writer has taken a view from a distance and noticed the pre-cast concrete forms decorating the face of the building. The second has recorded the experience of entering the library. Neither image-list is poetic. Both, however, have a certain clarity and physical definition.

The making of image-lists is one of the earliest recorded aspects of poetry. When we make a list of this kind, or make a picture, or record an event, we do so because we feel, instinctively, that to picture something is to control it and preserve it. The writers of charms and spells felt the same way. They even felt that they could make something happen by describing the wished for event in words or pictures. If the spell or charm did not succeed in its purpose it was, they thought, because the words were in the wrong order, or lacked power for some other reason. The amount of spirit put into the words mattered. In reciting a charm (or prayer or incantation) one had to use a special type of breath, a special voice. In other words, the spell-makers felt that the effective poem should not only list all the essential elements of the event it wished to control, but also have a diction appropriate to the spell.

It is useful to think of making a poem in this way. How, for example, would one write a spell to ensure that one caught a fish, or discovered gold, or even fell asleep? One must describe all the essential sensations, and in the right tone of voice. If a group of people meets together to tackle this problem they can often decide on the essential elements in the wished-for event. It is a good way of selecting imagery. Then, however, each one must make his own spell. Here are two spells, one from the Navaho Indians, and one made by a student.

Hunting Song

Comes the deer to my singing,
Comes the deer to my song,
Comes the deer to my singing.

He, the blackbird, he am I,
Bird beloved of the wild deer.
        Comes the deer to my singing.

From the Mountain Black,
From the summit,
Down the trail, coming, coming, now,
        Comes the deer to my singing.

Through the blossoms,
Through the flowers, coming, coming now,
        Comes the deer to my singing.

Through the pollen, flower pollen,
        Coming, coming now,
        Comes the deer to my singing.

Starting with his left fore-foot,
Stamping, turns the frightened deer,
        Comes the deer to my singing.

Quarry mine, blessed am I
In the luck of the chase.
        Comes the deer to my singing.

        Comes the deer to my singing,
        Comes the deer to my song,
        Comes the deer to my singing.[1]

Spell for Spearing Salmon
To the mouth of the Klinakini
O spirit of the Salmon,
I take my spear
With its two prongs
One long
      one short,
With its pitch
With its line
With its stone point
With its bone barb.
At the mouth of the Klinakini,
Souls of the Salmon people,
I throw the salmon bones,

[1] Navaho song from *The Sky Clears, Poetry of the American Indians*, by A. Grove Day, University of Nebraska Press, 1951, p. 80.

All of them
    into the river.
The backbones,
The long bones,
The short bones,
The tail
    the eyes
      the head.
At the mouth of the Klinakini,
O spirit of the Salmon
Let the Salmon Child again be whole.

In making spells we are slowly approaching poetry proper, and getting a notion of the fundamental importance of selecting the right details and arranging them in the right order. Moreover, just as in the spell one must not allow doubt to intrude or even allow negative expressions that might produce a feeling in the fish, or the river god, or whoever, that there is even the slightest possibility of things not going smoothly, so in a poem one must not allow elements that counteract the poem's movement and tone.

The tone of a poem is partly controlled by its diction and partly by its imagery. A poem can be given much of its order and force by its selection and arrangement of images, as we have seen from William Carlos Williams' poem, *Nantucket*. In order to develop our ability to organize patterns of imagery it is helpful to practice several exercises. The first is based upon the notion that, as images are words which suggest physical sensation, they can be arranged according to the senses to which they most obviously refer. Some words, such as *harsh*, can refer equally to hearing and touch; some, like *sharp*, are used as often of hearing and taste as of touch. It is possible to group images together in such a way that, while the words relating to one sense may refer us also to others, the whole piece of writing runs the gamut of physical sensation.

This is most easily achieved by placing the speaker of a poem in a situation where he or she only gradually approaches a given phenomenon. First it is seen, then heard, then smelt, tasted, or touched. For the purpose of the exercise, and because the vocabulary of sight and sound is more extensive than the others, we may lump taste, smell, and touch together. Because taste, smell, and touch involve a closer contact than sight or hearing, this means that the poem mounts to a climax by way of a progression of images. Of course, in order to make a poem out of this exercise it has to be treated fairly freely; a too rigid adherence to the rules would make the progression seem too automatic. An illustration of the kind of progression that can, however, be managed is the following student exercise.

In the Library

Pink sweaters blurring into mottled air.
Crystal dangling there from her ear.
Lost. In green shirts and black umbrellas,
brown eyes, green eyes, coat creases,
the fingernail lying in the corner of the desk,
the unlighted exit sign.

The bouncing dust hits the tile. Heart . . .
heart? Beating.
Voices paper bags laughter
whisper while the chairs slide.
Creaks.
Footsteps close by me, the clanging of
coat hangers, of bells?

No. The desk is here. It sleeps under my fingers.
Warm skin. There is a draft coming from
somewhere. What was it like to lie on the grass?
I . . . can't . . . remember.

Flip the pages. These are fresh books, palpitating
with scented ideas. Not peppermint.
Not roses.
My clothes are wet grass in the morning.
My tongue reaches out to stone.

This poem reveals the way in which the exercise can lead to an almost hallucinatory intensity. The student originally called the poem *Dying in the Library*, in an effort to interpret the experience provided by the exploration to which the images led her.

Another type of progression is revealed in the next exercise.

The Five

'We're sorry, you'll have to get out of here.'
The five figures came closer
And he felt terribly alone,
Not sun nor warm vinyl comforted him.
There was nowhere else to go.

Their empty shoes scuffed the new pile.
He heard the rustle and stifling chafe
Of five conservative grey suits
With quiet ties knocking white-ulcered chests
With each step . . . a dull tattoo.

He let go of the moist arm. A paper, his own,
Threaded between his chair and the table.
It scraped his ankle . . . knife sharp,
He pressed his elbow to his ribs
To stop the cold drops from reaching his belt.

They took their seats, they knew their place,
He saw that they were done with him.
Complete dismissal, concave cheeks,
And one that chewed his nails.
A Swiss cigar, and eyes like guillotines.

The tobaccoed air numbed his sense,
Black vinyl almost bubbled in a sun
Made hot by winter. The smell of warm and then,
One of them spat . . . the sound of nail on tin . . .
And his fear was lost in the stench.

Here the first stanza is visual, apart from the word warm. The second
stanza is auditory apart from the words *grey* and *white*. The third stanza
is tactile throughout. The fourth stanza is again visual, and the last
stanza deals largely with the sense of smell, though there are visual and
auditory elements.

Another example of the results of concentrating upon sensual imagery
reveals a similar mysterious and nightmare progression.

The Bells

Said Y 'I saw them ring the bells
And in corduroy trousers and sweaters too—
Heaving up and down on the ropes.'
('The biggest bell weighed two tons,' he added)
But he could not taste God in the stone of the belfry;
He could only taste his own dry mouth.

Once, with courage, he touched a bell rope—
Felt the coarse cording cool under his hands
And saw a chance of being swung up
To Heaven or Hell if he hung on;
But he begged forgiveness for his ineptness
And sat down again to listen to the frost on the windows.

But Y heard through the silence of the frost
the crashing carillon and
Said to himself 'They sound very brave
But I can see the gargoyles laughing—a stone faced laugh.'
He touched his own gargoyle face and it was cold.

'Must we climb down those narrow stairs ?
It's rather dark' he quavered,
And he smelled bat droppings
And the odour of mice as he
Touched his damp hands to the railing
To feel the dry wood.

I always said afterwards
'The bells sounded so close to God,
And the smell of the tower was
Infinitely sweeter than an apple wood fire.'
'But, of course,' he remarked to a friend
'Belfries are no novelty to me.'

Such exercises may not result in poems, but they do result in our
becoming aware that, in writing poetry, we must arrange our imagery
so that the pattern of its sensual references is a part of the poem's overall
structure.

The five senses exercise is, of course, only a beginning. It can be
followed up with another in which the progression is organized in
terms of a movement from the gentle and vague to the harsh and concrete. The first stanza of such a poem includes words like *soft, cloud, mist,
dim, faint*; the second might make use of more definite words such as
blue, wet, green, smooth; and the third might involve the words *hard, sharp,
stone, black, white*. This poem progresses not only in terms of a decreasing
vagueness, but in terms of an increasing series of contrasts. The contrast
between black and white is bold; that between blue and green is not.

There are a number of progression games one can play, for there are
many ways in which imagery can be varied. It is easy to think up new
approaches.

These exercises, do more, however, than show us how to arrange
imagery for dramatic, or obsessive effect. They also impress upon us the
importance of seeing the different intensities of imagery. Some images
are diffuse, rather vague, and not at all dramatic. Others are vivid.
Some suggest, immediately, particular concrete shapes; others do not.
Moreover, some immediately involve us in ideas of physical sensation

and some only remind us vaguely of them. Thus the phrase *the long day* is diffuse in imagery. The noun refers to no one particular sense, and would be almost an abstraction if it were not referred to our partly physical sense of time by its accompanying adjective. That adjective, however, is also diffuse for it is largely descriptive of time, and only secondarily indicative of physical measurement. The phrase *the long road*, however, is more immediate in its physical reference, and the phrase *the long knife*, because the word knife suggests an even more limited shape than the word road, is the most immediate and concrete of the three.

In general, it is wise to make the fullest possible use of concrete and immediate imagery, for it reminds the reader of the physical presence of the speaker of the poem; he is not a disembodied intellect or computer-like observer; he is, like us, a sensual being. 'No poetry' said William Carlos Williams, 'save in things'. I would, I think, rewrite this as 'No poetry save through the senses' and remind you that William Blake once called the five senses 'the chief inlets of Soul in this Age'.

Most young poets find it hard to use immediate and concrete imagery. They wish to say something about *the soul*, or *the spirit*, and their poems are filled with abstractions like *Truth*, or such words as *Love* which, being largely abstract, only have physical connotations of a generalized kind. This is partly because they want to *say something* and to tell us *about* something. They therefore use the language of interpretation and commentary rather than that of recreation. It is necessary to emphasize that a poem should not talk about beauty or sadness or loneliness but present images, physical references, that create the emotions required. This is what T. S. Eliot meant when he talked about the *objective correlative* and said:

> The only way of expressing emotion in the form of art is by finding an 'objective correlative'; in other words, a set of objects, a situation, a chain of events which shall be the formula of that particular emotion; such that when the external facts, which must terminate in sensory experience, are given, the emotion is immediately evoked.
>
> *Hamlet* (1919)

Learning to reduce the number of abstractions in one's work is difficult. There is, however, one exercise that helps. This is to take a number of words descriptive of emotion and then attempt to list the objects which might cause those emotions, or which do cause those emotions in oneself. I have sometimes startled my students by asking them to write down the dozen most disgusting images they can imagine. Several usually find themselves putting down images which appear quite innocuous to others, words like *mud* or *frog* or *tapioca*. In arriving at these words, however, they have been obliged to analyse exactly what it is that most disgusts them, and have found out something about themselves as well as provided a useful word hoard for their work. Hunting the objective correlative is always, however, a frustrating business, and the quarry most usually escapes. As in so many of these exercises it is the doing of the exercises that is important; only rarely are the results of value to any but the student concerned.

The arrangement of verbal excitements is not only a matter of selecting the nearest thing to an objective correlative that one can find, or selecting immediate images rather than abstractions and organizing them into a pattern. It is often also a matter of finding something in the nature of a narrative structure or poetic *plot*. A poem exists in time; it progresses. It does not matter how many wonderful immediate images, how many magnificent associative leaps, or how many original perceptions you have achieved if you have not got an onward moving plot to sustain them.

Of course, in the majority of cases, one does not know much about the plot of one's poem. One has a notion that if one starts off with a particular *given* line, or with a vivid image, the poem will develop its own progressing pattern. Indeed, if one knows too much about the poem one is writing one may block out all those happy creative accidents and surprising images that make a poem worth having. Nevertheless, whether it occurs consciously or quite unconsciously, the internal dialogue at the onset of a poem may well go something like this:

A: I've got all these great feelings about cats. What can I do with them?

B: Be a bit more precise, for a start. What 'great feelings'?

A: Well, they interest me. They are so independent, and aloof, and yet so affectionate. And their hair is filled with electricity. And their eyes shine in the dark. And they are both sophisticated and primitive.

B: Are you trying to write an essay or a poem?

A: A poem, of course.

B: Well, then, look for the images that have the most possibility of being exploited, and that refer outwards to universal notions.

A: You mean like cruelty, sophistication, cunning, elegance—that sort of thing?

B: Yes. But you can't just gossip, you know! Where do you see your cat?

A: Well, in a jungle, a forest, in the wilds.

B: I can't see why, but that's fair enough. What are you doing in the forest?

A: I'm camping. In a clearing. The cat is at the edge of the clearing.

B: What happens?

A: Well, I try to feed it, I guess. It has some scraps I give it. It's affectionate. I think it's lost.

B: Is it?

A: I don't know. Oh yes, I do. It's obviously a stray domestic cat run wild—but still domestic enough to take food from my hand.

B: Hand?

A: Saucer, then.

B: So what happens? We need a bit of a surprise you know! So far this could go in the Cat-Lover's Gazette.

A: Well, it is evening, I guess. It grows dark. And it goes back to the forest.

B: So?

A: Everything's different. I get up to have a pee, or tighten a guy rope or something and there it is—watching me—two eyes burning in the night.

B: Forget about William Blake.

A: I have.

B: What's the point, then?

A: Well, the way in which domestic animals—domestic feelings perhaps —aren't what they seem. All that politeness disguises a beast. You know, I'm feeling suddenly less affectionate about cats—more uneasy.

B: That's a good sign.

A: Anyway it's got some kind of a story now. Maybe I can write it. How about starting with

'From the edge of the forest suddenly a cat,
Elegant, sinuous, putting foot before foot
Exquisitely as a dancer . . .'

B: See you later!

I won't produce the poem. I haven't written it yet, and in any case the dialogue has already made the point I wanted to make. In finding your narrative, your poetic plot, you start by saying, 'When did it happen? Where did it happen?' Then you don't say exactly, 'What happened?' but 'What if it happened that . . . ?' and always pick the situation that opens up more possibilities than it shuts out. To write poetry is to work with a succession of expanding possibilities. Keep the thing on the move until some kind of pattern is formed, and you sense a certain finality of viewpoint.

The poetic plot, like, perhaps, the fiction plot, presents a series of events or pseudo-events, each one of which opens up further possibilities, until a dénouement becomes inevitable. There are several basic poetic plots. The most simple is that consisting of a series of variations, each one adding a new dimension to the subject matter, until it becomes clear that further addition would result in the poem becoming overloaded. This type of poem can best be illustrated by folk poetry, where the variations are simple and the objective correlatives obvious. In the Mahi Lament collected and translated by Ulli Beier, the various images of sorrow are clear and intelligible, and each new one adds more to our understanding of the scene in which the sorrow is felt.

Lament

Listen to my sorrow
listen to my lament.
The bat was struck by misfortune
its head is hanging low.
I too was struck by misfortune
my arms are hanging limp.
The monkey was struck by misfortune
his brothers cease their play.
The lake is full of water
the lake cannot move away.
The room where we are drinking
the room has become dark.
The forest has burst into flames
the hyena looks for its mother.

> The antelope flees the forest
> the antelope's life is sad.
> Listen to my sorrow
> listen to my lament.[1]

This type of variation is seen at its most sophisticated in such poems as Wallace Stevens's *Thirteen Ways of Looking at a Blackbird*, and at its most obvious in Elizabeth Barrett Browning's sonnet, *How do I love you? Let me count the ways*. It is also, however, part of the poetic plot of some more substantial poems, such as Goldsmith's *The Deserted Village*, Johnson's *The Vanity of Human Wishes*, and Swift's *Ode on the Death of Doctor Swift*. In some of these the poetic plot is given greater interest by being attached to a notion of a man conducting a survey; the personality of the speaker is a part of the plot, and his developing viewpoint, his shifting vision, also follows a progression.

Variation Plot is often combined with the second type of plot, Dialectic Plot. This derives its interest from its use of debate, or statement and counter-statement. A brief analysis of a Shakespeare sonnet from this point of view may illustrate the method. The poet begins his poem:

> Shall I compare thee to a summer's day ?

The answer to this question could be either 'Yes' or 'No'. If it is 'Yes', then the poet may find himself obliged to discuss the lady entirely in terms of summer imagery. If the answer is 'No', then, in explaining why not, he can use the imagery of summer and other imagery also. The answer 'No', moreover, establishes a tension in the poem and obliges him to defend his refusal.

> Thou art more lovely and more temperate.

This can be elaborated upon. In what way is she more lovely and more temperate ?

> Rough winds do shake the darling buds of May
> And summer's lease hath all too short a date.

This could end the poem, but it may be worth while to elaborate upon the metaphorical use of the notion of a short lease and show how it applies to summer.

---

[1] A Mahi lament collected and translated by Ulli Beier, and published in his *African Poetry, an Anthology of Traditional African Poems*, Cambridge University Press, 1966.

Sometimes too hot the eye of heaven shines,
And often is his gold complexion dimm'd:
And every fair from fair sometimes declines,
By chance or nature's changing course untrimm'd.

The poem cannot end here, for the last statement opens more doors than it closes. In what way can the lady's beauty be regarded as not subject to nature's changing course? Is this in fact what he means us to believe? Is this the essential difference between the lady and the summer day? We demand an explanation, and we get one.

But thy eternal summer shall not fade,
Nor lose possession of that fair thou owest;
Nor shall death brag thou wander'st in his shade
When in eternal lines to time thou grow'st.

What lines? What does the man mean?

So long as men can breathe, or eyes can see,
So long lives this, and this gives life to thee.

The resolution is achieved. It is worth noticing that in this poem Shakespeare did not choose the Image-Association progress which Christina Rossetti used for her stanza on a similar theme of mortal decay. He chose a dialectic method, and his imagery has no clear progression, though lines 9–12 involve images of darkness and shade rather than the brighter images of the first six lines. This is, however, more a contrast between the two parts of the poem than a progression.

It may be thought that the dialectic method is only appropriate to short and neatly stanzaic poems, and perhaps especially appropriate to sonnets. It cannot be denied that the Shakespearean sonnet makes this particular poetic plot, if not inevitable, at least very likely, but there are many other longer poems of other periods and in other languages which use the same basic method.

Take, for example, the opening stanzas of Thomas Hardy's *Who's in the Next Room?* Here the Dialectic Plot is at its simplest: the poem is a dialogue.

'Who's in the next room?—who?
I seemed to see
Somebody in the dawning passing through,
Unknown to me.'
'Nay: you saw nought. He passed invisibly.'

'Who's in the next room?—who?
            I seem to hear
Somebody muttering firm in a language new
            That chills the ear.'
'No: you catch not his tongue who has entered there.'

'Who's in the next room?—who?
            I seem to feel
His breath like a clammy draught, as if it drew
            From the Polar Wheel.'
'No: none who breathes at all does the door conceal.'

'Who's in the next room?—who?
            A figure wan
With a message to one in there of something due?
            Shall I know him anon?'
'Yea, he; and he brought such; and you'll know him anon.'

Notice how the last line of each stanza leaves the problem unsolved, so that a further stanza is inevitable, and we can be given further details of the situation. Slowly, we begin to understand it. As well as being an illustration of the use of dialogue, this poem also shows the value of the Unanswered Question manœuvre, and gives us another example of a poem built on sensual progression. The movement is from how the speaker sees, through how he hears and feels to what he knows, or does not know. The Unanswered Question plot is, of course, another basic one. It is the notion upon which the whole of Walter de la Mare's poem, *The Listeners*, is based. It is also present in Robert Graves's *Welsh Incident*, Robert Browning's *My Last Duchess*, Blake's *Tyger Tyger*, and countless other poems of all periods and cultures.

The unanswered question and the dialogue are both methods of creating suspense. We want to have our questionings answered. The poem has opened up territories we feel we must explore. Poems must create suspense. They need not always do it by dialogue or the presentation of a mystery, however. They can do it by beginning with an assertion so idealistic, challenging, or inconclusive that the reader cannot accept it without saying 'So what?' Consider the following two poems, one by the second-century Chinese poet Ts'ao Chih, translated by J. D. Frodsham and published in *An Anthology of Chinese Verse* (O.U.P. 1967), and one by Walter de la Mare.

In the south country there lives a lovely lady,
Her face delicate as peach or plum.
In the morning she wanders on the north shore of the River,
In the evening she wanders on an islet in the Hsiang.
But these days rosy cheeks are out of fashion,
No one is there to see her dazzling smile.
In the blink of an eye, the year's night is on us,
Such fleeting beauty cannot last for long.

Ts'ao Chih

Here lies a most beautiful lady,
Light of step and heart was she;
I think she was the most beautiful lady
That ever was in the West Country.

But beauty vanishes; beauty passes;
However rare—rare it be;
And when I crumble, who will remember
This lady of the West Country?

Walter de la Mare

I have now outlined a number of basic poetic plots: the Variations Plot, The Dialectic Plot, the Question Plot, and the Contrast Plot. If we add to these the Image Progression Plot described earlier, and, obviously, the straight Narrative Plot, we have six of the most basic poetic plots in front of us.

In order to learn how to think in terms of these plots, however, we need to practise using them. This requires very little ingenuity. The Variations Plot can be practised merely by following the pattern of the Mahi poem, taking a particular emotion and listing instances or events which are immediately associable with that emotion. The Dialectic Plot and Dialogue Plot can be learned as if they were the same by inventing a dialogue between two people whose view of the nature or attractiveness of some event is opposed. This also teaches the Contrast Plot. The Question Plot is just as easy to find an exercise for. All one needs to do is pose a question in line one, and make sure that the final line of the paragraph or stanza presents an enigma which makes a following question necessary. Poetic Plots, however, are not the only necessities for giving the poem a progression and a meaningful shape. Verse form itself can be a kind of plot, carrying one forward because of devices of rhythm and repetition. If we are to get any further with studying the practice of poetry we must start looking at the verse form, at elementary prosody, and the uses of rhyme.

THREE The Basics of Verse

The fundamentals of verse form are extremely easy to understand, once they have been pointed out, but are very rarely taught. Teachers tend to introduce their pupils to quite sophisticated forms right at the beginning, and these are difficult to imitate. The forms of nursery rhymes are not as simple as one might suppose. If you doubt this, I suggest that you try to imitate exactly the rhythm and rhyme scheme of *Mary Mary Quite Contrary*, *Hickory Dickory Dock*, or *Mary Had A Little Lamb*, and see how far you can get without being trapped into absurdity by the exigencies of rhyme or metre. There are, as a matter of fact, very few really simple verses in English. Even our earliest recorded literature is extremely highly wrought, and, moreover, as it is written in Anglo-Saxon few of us can read it. In order to look at basic verse form we are therefore obliged to turn to folk poems from other countries, and to some of the simpler kinds of children's word games,

If we do this we discover immediately that the basic characteristic common to primitive poetry is the repetition of sound effects. These may take the form of repeating a simple pattern of accented and un-accented syllables; of repeating vowel sounds, or consonants, or vowel-consonant combinations; or of repeating words, phrases, and syntactical constructions. These repetitions give one the impression that the message being delivered has a pattern, and because we are always im-pressed by tidy arrangement, and have apparently an inbuilt disposition to be persuaded of the authority and truth of something that is well ordered and clearly designed, we regard such messages as being *special*, and we are excited by them and admire them.

The majority of children's word games and nursery rhymes are far from simple. There is, however, one type of children's poetry which shows the fundamentals of verse form clearly enough. This is that popular and internationally known type of catalogue poetry that in-cludes *The House that Jack Built*, *The Farmer in the Dell*, and the following:

Monday's child is fair of face,
Tuesday's child is full of grace,
Wednesday's child is full of woe,
Thursday's child has far to go,
Friday's child is loving and giving,
Saturday's child works hard for a living,
And the child that is born on the Sabbath Day
Is bonny and blithe and good and gay.

The method here is simple enough. We repeat a simple syntactical formula six times and then we vary it to conclude the poem. There is a West African children's song from Akan that follows exactly the same method. It was first published by Kwabena Nketia in the third number of the magazine *Orpheus*. It is a lullaby.

Someone would like to have you for her child
but you are mine.
Someone would like to rear you on a costly mat
but you are mine.
Someone would like to place you on a camel blanket
but you are mine.
I have to rear you on a torn old mat.
Someone would like to have you as her child
but you are mine.

A Uraon poem from India uses the same technique, this time without climactic variation, for the poem itself comes to narrative climax.

Within the garden a tank is dug
Seven wives wash with the seven brothers
Ankle deep the tank is dug
Seven wives wash with the seven brothers
Knee deep the tank is dug
Seven wives wash with the seven brothers
Thigh deep the tank is dug
Seven wives wash with the seven brothers
Waist deep the tank is dug
Seven wives wash with the seven brothers
Chest deep the tank is dug
Seven wives wash with the seven brothers
Neck deep the tank is dug
Seven wives wash with the seven brothers

Europe, Africa, and India can all produce the same poetic formula. What about America ?

Here is a poem by the Navaho.

> The first man—you are his child, he is your child.
> The first woman—you are his child, he is your child.
> The water monster—you are his child, he is your child.
> The black sea-horse—you are his child, he is your child.
> The black snake—you are his child, he is your child.
> The big blue snake—you are his child, he is your child.
> The white corn—you are his child, he is your child.
> The yellow corn—you are his child, he is your child.
> The corn pollen—you are his child, he is your child.
> The corn beetle—you are his child, he is your child.
> Sahanahray—you are his child, he is your child.
> Bekayhozhon—you are his child, he is your child.

These two last poems are both, of course, ritual chants, and may be regarded as very primitive poetry indeed. Let us, however, look at fragments of obviously sophisticated poetry in which the same formula is used.

> I see a great round wonder rolling through space,
> I see diminutive farms, hamlets, ruins, graveyards, jails,
>   factories, palaces, hovels, huts of barbarians, tents
>   of nomads upon the surface,
> I see the shaded part on one side where the sleepers are
>   sleeping, and the sunlit part on the other side,
> I see the curious rapid change of the light and shade,
> I see distant lands, as real and near to the inhabitants
>   of them as my land is to me.
>   Walt Whitman, *Salut Au Monde!*

> I remember, when I was a boy,
> I heard the scream of a frog, which was caught with his foot
>   in the mouth of an upstarting snake;
> I remember when I first heard bull-frogs break into sound in
>   the spring;
> I remember hearing a wild goose out of the throat of night
> Cry loudly, beyond the lake of waters;
> I remember the first time, out of a bush in the darkness, a
>   nightingale's piercing cries and gurgles startled the
>   depths of my soul;
> I remember the scream of a rabbit as I went through a wood
>   at midnight . . .
>   D. H. Lawrence, *Tortoise Shout*

Tomorrow is that lamp upon the marsh, which a traveller never
  reacheth;
Tomorrow, the rainbow's cup, coveted prize of ignorance;
Tomorrow, the shifting anchorage, dangerous trust of mariners;
Tomorrow, the wrecker's beacon, wily snare of the destroyer.
Reconcile convictions with delay, and To-morrow is a fatal lie!
Frighten resolutions into action, To-morrow is a wholesome
  truth;
I must, for I fear To-morrow; this is the Cassava's food;
Why should I? let me trust To-morrow,—this is the Cassava's
  poison

Martin Tupper, Of Tomorrow

Yesterday all the past. The language of size
Spreading to China along the trade-routes; the diffusion
  Of the counting-frame and the cromlech;
Yesterday the shadow-reckoning in the sunny climates.

Yesterday the assessment of insurance by cards,
The divination of water; yesterday the invention
  Of cartwheels and clocks, the taming of
Horses. Yesterday the bustling world of the navigators.

W. H. Auden, Spain 1937

I have given you hands which you turn from worship,
I have given you speech, for endless palaver,
I have given you my Law, and you set up commissions,
I have given you lips, to express friendly sentiments,
I have given you hearts, for reciprocal distrust,
I have given you power of choice, and you only alternate
Between futile speculation and unconsidered action.

T. S. Eliot, The Rock

If this formula is one of the basic ones perhaps we ought to begin with
it. Let us try an exercise which will make use of the formula. I have set
my students one which usually has good effects. This consists of writing
seven sentences of the same length, none long. The first three are to
begin with the word *Stone*. The second three are not to include the word
Stone and the last sentence is to begin again with the word *Stone*. Sometimes I have used *Water* or *Fire* instead of stone. Here are some of the
results.

I

Stone is rather dense
Stone can be seen
Stone on the ground

The grass is green
Ralph is a dog
How high is up

Stone is where you find it.

2

Stone can be carved by knives
Stone walls are not necessarily physical
Stone books do not have any pages

There are gigantic birds on the lamp
Twist the arm 'til it breaks
Work hard and delude yourself with success.

Stone images are empty gods.

3

Stone-sized beads in a string
Stone finds its way into a painting
Stone can change shape at dusk.

The floor is patterned and destroys perspective
Guns help commit murder
The moss on a tree hangs on the north side

Stone becomes the basis for many houses.

In writing these formula-poems, the students find themselves, towards the end, happening upon ideas that surprise them. Fantasy replaces logic and factual observation. This is caused partly by boredom with the factual and obvious and partly by conscious or unconscious recognition of the ancestry of the form in magic. Another similar exercise involves the making of a series of statements, each of similar length, which begin with the first person and a verb. This is the pattern of much folk poetry. Again, the list produces surprises, for fantasy has to replace logic. The mind strays into fantasy when it becomes bored and as the formal organization, the surface of the writing, is so simple and childlike, the result is usually an escape into the imaginative. If we examine these exercises we soon discover that in most cases the sentences are not only of similar length, but also similar in rhythm. We judge length (unless we are pedantic and count syllables) by the number of emphatic verbal effects per line, only adjusting this when the line appears to move faster or more slowly than usual.

The best way to start developing a sense of form is, apart from reading poetry, to think of one's writing in units of length, and to create paragraphs (call them verse or prose) in which the proportions are all similar. Thus one can alternate short and long verbal units, create patterns in which the units gradually increase or decrease in length, and then move on to more elaborate patterns. It is unwise to measure the lengths too accurately and clinically; one's own ear and sense of timing is a better guide than syllable or word counting. If one adds to this Proportional Verse (if it is verse—for we are now on the border between verse and prose) some other devices of repetition, the result can have real formal strength. Consider the following student exercise, which follows a very simple formula indeed. Each paragraph consists of a statement beginning with the name of the protagonist, Sammy. This is then followed by another statement. To begin with each paragraph is composed of only two statements. In the fourth and fifth paragraphs there is a slight amount of variation. The sixth and last paragraph returns to the basic formula.

Sammy

Sammy, his ears bleeding, paused while they
bayed. The pack was near, circling in loose earth,
they aspired to climb trees,—to drop and cling.

Sammy, you mad dog, run if you can! Their
purpose was clear, they would place him in a chest and
bury him under a stake.

Sammy, caught in a sponge, struggled while his
arms peeled and cesspools foamed. He would be
drowned in a bin of poppies in Saunder's field.

Sammy, now in a panic, chewed his way to
sunlight and found everything calm. Smiling he rid
his nostrils of flower dust. Blow boy Blow!

Sammy, falsely reassured, played his harp for
the sparrows as a light breeze flitted. The trees
stood still; everything paused as greens, blues and
whites—Could no one warn him?

Sammy, now naked and exposed, cried as they
galloped over him and left him for dead. Don't cry
Sammy, it was bound to happen—beautiful hoof-cloven
head!

A variation upon this exercise consists of simply utilizing initial repetition of a more or less meaningless word or verbal noise. Here are examples using letters.

L

L inhabits the mystical square on the tile floor.
L hides in the leaf shuffling across the sidewalk.
L commands from light bulbs with total perception.
L looks out from the Russian alphabet and mocks.
L is the colour of the orange peel in the ashtray.
L moves under the eyes sliding as they turn.
L divides the lovers into two.
L is between the toes and loves to laugh.
L loves to laugh.

M

M abides.
M endures.
M is ignored by the evil ones, but thwarts them.
M gives the thirteenth gift, changing death to sleep.
M brings sleep to children lost in the forest.
M relieves you, whispers that you are dreaming.
M abides.
M endures.
M will not be summoned, bidden or placated.
M appears only in the pain brought by the evil ones.
M is the end of that pain, is the antidote kiss.
M shows you beauty in the beast and in the witch's tower.
M abides.
M endures.
M knows all secret names, and reveals them at need.
M forges all magic blades, and provides them at need.
M weaves all saving spells, and whispers them at need.
M survives all evil ones, and banishes them at need.
M abides.
M endures.

Another version of this exercise involves contrasting short with long paragraphs, and giving only the short paragraphs the repetitive opening. Within the longer paragraphs, however, several words recur. *But, Then* are two of them. Other pattern-making devices are also used. The short paragraphs follow the name of the protagonist on each occasion with parenthetical statements.

William

William (who had a seashell for a navel), watched the
storm blundering in from the West.

'Get away' they said, 'Get away!'

But he went on picking up crabs and putting them
safely under rocks. The rocks were red and the crabs
yellow and William would pause now and then to play his
silver flute in praise of such colour. Then he took off
his shoes and admired his webbed toes. They were turning grey.
'Good', he thought, 'for timing is essential.'

William (his speech now gone), sniffed the blue wind.
'Don't be a fool' they cried, 'don't be a fool!'

But he turned his back and stroked the fur on his arms.
It was a rich brown and he laughed as his arms shrunk and
nestled close to his chest. Then he took off his clothes and
lay down on his belly. And when the first scorching waves
climbed the beach William touched his whiskers to the
foam, drank deeply and swam away from shore.

William (his teeth now sharp as needles), dove for the
bottom.
'You're in the wrong house' they shouted, 'You're
in the wrong house!' and tried to pluck the seashell
from his navel. But he struck at them with his flipper
and bit a hermit crab in two to teach it a lesson. Then
he rolled over and over in the waves. They were his
mother's breasts and they showered him with milk. Then
William swam to shore to feast on the yellow crabs under
the red rocks.

'Timing is everything' he thought.

William is more elaborate than *Sammy*. Both use narrative plot, of course,
and both use proportional verse and repetition. But the second varies the
formula more extensively.

The kind of formula one chooses for exercises like this can to a very
considerable extent determine, if not the precise subject matter, then
certainly the tone, and therefore the vision of the poem. One might, for
example decide to compose one's proportional verse by using units of
three lines, the third line being shorter than the preceding two.

The blue harbour wrinkled the light between stone walls.
The white gulls were knives of light carving the air.
The boats rocked idly.

The afternoon brooded over its peace like a dreamy woman.
The hands of the houses were folded together and still.
The windows shivered.

The windows shivered to feel the pressures of stillness.
The rigging shivered to feel the beginnings of wind.
The dream was over.

No matter how hard one tries, in making this, using this formula one
finds that it is sooner or later the third line that is the main vehicle of
the poem's aggression. This particular formula is, of course, quite close
to the formula of orthodox *Sapphics*,[1] such as these by John Heath-Stubbs.

O Muse, descent now, Cinderella goddess—
If not to my lips, yet descend, astounding
(Lambent with terrors, or in clear compassion)
    These sand-blind English!

Cataract, come down—or as cat-o'-nine-tails—
Striking the waves of Isis, Usk, and Duddon,
Since in their reed-beds geese are counted swans now,
    Kestrels, gyrfalcons.

Cloud-signs are ill-set; light departs—permit not
We should allow the things your wings had taught us,
As in a dream's shame, utterly to vanish,
    Through keeping silence.
      John Heath-Stubbs, *Sapphic Ode.*
       Concluding stanzas.

In these English sapphics, the metrical pattern demands that each stanza
end with an unstressed syllable. It is interesting to take this hint and
use a formula which involves the repetition of a rhythmic device of this
kind. Take, first of all, the simple use of unstressed line endings.

There is a small child in the garden,
holding a pebble between his thumb and finger.
His eyes are blue; his hair is long and curly.
He walks upright with a kind of drunken stumble.
As I watch him he turns and stares at my window,
and I wonder if in the future he will imagine
the spectacle of a poet engaged in writing
this simple exercise for the sake of practice.

[1] See page 161.

This deliberately dull and artificial illustration makes a point worth making. When one reads it through one suspects rhyme, and yet this is not the case. In fact, if one repeats a rhythmic unit at the close of successive lines of roughly similar length the reader will sense a degree of regularity that does not in fact exist.

Writing in this way leads one on inevitably to more regular rhythmic composition, because one learns to adjust the tune of one's speech, the natural rise and fall of the voice, to accommodate given rhythmical units without strain. One learns this very slowly. The step after writing lines, or paragraphs, in which one rhythmic device is repeated, is to attempt lines or paragraphs involving more than one rhythmic similarity.

Let us suggest an exercise in which there are two repeated rhythmic characteristics; let us suggest that each line has a pause in the middle and ends with an accented syllable preceded by an unaccented one. This is easy enough to do.

> Was he ever here ? Or has he gone ?
> Ask the neighbours. They don't reply.
> Is he alive ? Or is he dead ?
> The road is empty. The house is still,
> and there in the mailbox, stiff and white,
> is the letter you sent, the debt you paid.

Let us then try beginning lines with similar rhythmic patterns. As long as we do not set ourselves, too soon, the task of writing octosyllabics, or iambic pentameter, we will find that our ability to work with organized rhythms steadily increases. After practising the repetition of rhythmic units, it is time to attend to the matter of line-length in a more precise manner than we have so far.

In English the best line to start with is, for most people, the four-stress line. The five-stress line reminds one's ear of blank verse and also appears to give the writer too much elbow-room. He begins to pad his statements out with adjectives. As the key words in any statement normally carry stress, the four-stress line means that if one has a noun and a verb one can only then afford one more noun and an adjective. In the five-stress line there is a terrible tendency to have one adjective for each of the two nouns, and even though one may use adverbs or make one's statements span two lines, the adjective-noun combination, if consistent, can become boring.

Of course, one man may scan a line differently from another; one man's four-stress line may be another's three- or five-stress line. This does not matter very much. We should not, at this stage, allow ourselves to become obsessed with technicalities. We are learning to handle the tools, not learning to use them to their fullest potential. We must walk before we can run.

It is at this point, however, that another problem emerges. Dividing one's writing up into lengths sometimes makes it difficult to say easily whatever comes into one's head.

Oddly enough, this problem becomes less intense if one gives oneself other tasks to perform at the same time. One of the difficulties about writing in a given stress-verse line, or, indeed, in a given metre, is that the form itself, while a good vehicle for expression, does not itself generate excitement or promote new approaches to one's material. It is, therefore, far easier to learn to write in stress-verse if one simultaneously attempts to create disciplined forms in that verse.

The most helpful forms are those which, because of their stanzaic structure, enable one to think easily in verse paragraphs. The four-line stanza is the most simple. A three-line stanza is also valuable, though it does not provide the same opportunity for the making of parallel statements. The longer the stanza the more difficult it is to retain dramatic intensity.

When practising these stanzaic forms most students find themselves, quite without intention, beginning to use rhyme. This is largely because the form demands additional strength, and rhyme can create chiming sound patterns that make even the least enterprising statements appear well ordered and poised.

Unfortunately, most students have very limited ideas of the possibilities of rhyme, and make their task more difficult than it need be by attempting only full or rich rhymes. As there is a limited supply of these, the poem becomes distorted by the necessity of finding rhyme-words. For those interested in exploring rhyme fully, and for those who find their imaginations respond to the challenge of technical problems, I have listed and commented upon the different kinds of rhyme and chiming devices in another part of this book.[1] Most readers, however, may feel that is enough to get a rough idea of the subject and that the provision of exact labels and categories is mere pedantry. This may be the case; nevertheless a clear understanding of rhyming devices is of real importance to the apprentice poet.

First of all let us agree to consider any use of repeated sounds as a

[1] See below, pp. 151–55.

kind of rhyme. If we start from this point we can see that much supposedly unrhymed verse derives strength and interest from its pattern
of sounds. The opening of Edward Thomas's *The Unknown Bird* makes
the point for us.

> Three lovely notes he whistled, too soft to be heard
> If others sang; but others never sang
> In the great beech-wood all that May and June.
> No one saw him: I alone could hear him
> Though many listened. Was it but four years
> Ago ? or five ? He never came again.

It is obvious that this is tuneful speech, and that the vowel sounds and
consonants produce a pleasing music. If we look closely at these sounds
we see that Thomas has used chiming (or rhyming) effects several times.
There are five *s* sounds in the first two lines. The word *sang* is repeated.
In the third line we have <u>M</u>ay a<u>nd</u> Ju<u>ne</u> and in the fourth the *m* is repeated
in the word *him* which is itself repeated, thus paralleling the kind of
repetition we found in the second line. The *n* sound is also repeated in
one and *alone*. The *m* and *n* sounds occur again in the fifth line in *many*
and *listened* and the verse paragraph ends with *n* after briefly reminding
us of the earlier soft *s* sounds with *listened*. The *s* sound here is first
used in describing the song of the bird; as soon as the poem reminds us
of the song we get the *s* of *listened*—not, as we might have done perhaps,
the *h*s and *m*s of *heard him* or the sounds of such other acceptable phrases
as *hoped to* or *wished to*. After this sound the next *s* is hard, in *was*, and then
there are no more soft *s* sounds but the hard *g* of *ago* and the hard *c* of
came, and the paragraph ends with one long vowel sound repeated,
almost mournfully, together with the *m* and *n* sounds that tied earlier
lines together. Now, looking over the piece again, we can see that the
music is largely based upon the repetition of *m* and *n* sounds with the
allied sound of *ng* and that this is relieved by the repeated *s*; we can now
also see that, while the poem is unrhymed the preponderance of *n*s and
*m*s makes the end-words *sang, June, him,* and *again* sufficiently noticeable
as sounds for their near-rhyming to be effective. The remaining two
end-words we can now see are also faintly, though very faintly chiming,
though perhaps as much to the eye as to the ear. *Heard* and *years* both
have long vowel sounds and muted *r* sounds.

This passage by Edward Thomas may look as if it were constructed
by a computer, or in some other way intellectually constructed. In all

probability, however, Thomas simply wrote the lines with close attention to the sounds they were making and did not analyse the exact pattern. The young poet learning to handle the music of speech would do well not to analyse his effects while constructing his verse, but rather listen to the sounds he is making and try to feel their appropriateness to the mood of the poem.

There are several exercises which can help the student to learn this kind of watchfulness. The first is to attempt to write nonsensical mood music, or mouth music. Let us attempt to produce a melancholy sound, for example. Such an attempt might result in:

the falling slowness of sombre weary dawn

It doesn't make much sense but the long vowel sounds make the line moan, the *ombre* of *sombre* demands a dwelling upon the *m* sound and slows up the line. It uses repeated *s* sounds and also repeats *w*.

Now let us try to produce a gay and cheerful sound. This could turn out to be:

the little twinkling bounce of bubbles

Lightness and speed is given the line by the short *i* sound and the tripping *l*s, and this tripping lightness is made more boisterous by the explosive repeated *b*s.

This exercise can, of course, be made just as complicated as one desires. One can, for example, suggest presenting a change of mood, either sudden or gradual.

The little twinklings in the sombre dawn

might do as a description of a lake in the early morning, for example.

If one concerns oneself too much with mouth music of course one can find oneself trapped into the sort of excesses which mar some of the poetry of Swinburne and Dylan Thomas. It is advisable to practise other exercises also if one is to learn other aspects of rhyming.

Let us consider the effect of truly rich and rigorous rhyming—the kind that young poets so often attempt and usually fail in achieving. Consider first of all these lines by John Clare.

> When midnight comes a host of dogs and men
> Go out and track the badger to his den,
> And put a sack within the hole, and lie
> Till the old grunting badger passes by.

He comes and hears—they let the strongest loose.
The old fox hears the noise and drops the goose.
The poacher shoots and hurries from the cry,
And the old hare half wounded buzzes by.
They get a forkèd stick to bear him down
And clap the dogs and take him to the town,
And bait him all the day with many dogs,
And laugh and shout and fright the scampering hogs.
He runs along and bites at all he meets:
They shout and hollo down the noisy streets.

This opening verse paragraph of Clare's *Badger* is rather pedestrian and dull even though the actions it describes are lively. One of the reasons for this is the relentless accuracy of the full rhyming; there is no variation or progression in it, and the last couplet which should produce a feeling of climax, fails to do so because the rhyming is no more or less intense than the previous rhyming. Why don't we maul Clare's poem about and try to make it have a more conversational flow and a more interesting rhyme progression? Let us start off with near-rhymes and allow ourselves a rich rhyme only at the end.

When midnight comes a host of dogs and men
Go out and track the badger to his home,
and put a sack within the hole, and wait
Till the old grunting badger lurches past.
He comes and hears—they let the strongest free.
The old fox hears the noise and drops his prey.
The poacher shoots and hurries from the cry
And the old hare, half wounded, starts away.
They get a forked stick to hold him firm
And clap the dogs and take him to the town,
And bait him all the day with many dogs
And laugh and shout and fright the scampering pigs;
He runs along and bites at all he meets:
They shout and hallo down the noisy streets.

This is still pedestrian, but the lines do not clang so much and the predictable nature of the couplet is qualified in the middle of the passage by four lines which group themselves together with variations upon final long vowel sounds—*free, prey, cry, away*. If we wanted to make the poem less stiff-limbed, however, we would have to alter the syntax and rhythm also, and we would certainly have to remove some of those *ands* to vary the pace of the speech.

The point of this exercise is to show how rhyme, when clangorously predictable, can prevent a poem from sounding at all excited or spontaneous. This is not always the case, of course. Pope and Dryden reveal how the heroic couplet can be made vivid and lively, and some lyrics derive wit and gaiety from their ingenuity in rhyme.

It is, of course, the timing of rhyme words that is important. If the poem's rhythm is such that the reader knows precisely when the rhyme is going to occur and exactly what kind of noise is going to be made he is not likely to be excited by the poem's music. Therefore the poet must never permit his poem to lose the element of surprise. He can surprise with half-rhymes or with full-rhymes; he can delay the arrival of the rhyme word, or he can place it earlier than expected. He can build up through near-rhymes to full rhymes, or he can interrupt full-rhymes with near-rhyming passages. Consider the following two pieces.

i

In Casterbridge there stood a noble pile
Wrought with pilaster, bay, and balustrade
In tactful times when shrewd Eliza swayed.—
It smiled the long street down for near a mile.

ii

In Casterbridge there stood a noble pile,
Wrought with pilaster, bay, and balustrade
In tactful times when shrewd Eliza swayed.—
    On burgher, squire, and clown
It smiled the long street down for near a mile.

The second passage is the first verse of Thomas Hardy's poem, *A Man*, as he published it; the first is my own revision of it. It must be obvious that my own version is less interesting. Long familiarity with poems in quatrains rhyming *abba* makes us anticipate that *ile* sound at the end of the fourth line. Hardy himself, however, frustrates our expectancy and enriches the poem with an unpredictable *clown/down* rhyme while delaying the arrival of the expected *ile* sound. As a consequence, we listen to the poem with more interest, and it is not until we have read several stanzas that we have grown familiar enough with this modification of an old tune to anticipate the timing of the rhyme words; by then, of course, we are paying sufficient attention to the poem's message not to be troubled, and Hardy himself makes things more pleasant for us by slightly varying the rhythm and speed so that our predictions are more often approximate than not.

To learn to write easily in rhyme it is necessary to practise a great deal. When I was a boy I used to make up rhyming stories as I walked along the country roads. I didn't much care if the stories made sense; I simply enjoyed the playing with rhyme. I would sometimes carry on a rambling rhymed narrative for a mile or more. This is one way to develop a quick ear so that one does not interrupt the flow of a poem in order to hunt out a rhyme. Another useful exercise is to work with the rhyme scheme *abcb*, that is to say with alternate rhyme, but deliberately to avoid making all the lines the same length or metrically regular. In this way one discovers for oneself that the essential element in good verse is not the metrical count but the timing, and one avoids falling into the trap of writing doggerel.

Nevertheless, however hard one tries to preserve one's freedom, and however freely one handles rhyme, it is at this point that the form of the verse begins to inhibit one's imagination. There is only one solution to this problem, and that is continual practice. There is no substitute for hard work. In order, however, to avoid suffering the most intense types of frustration, you should make a distinction between writing exercises and writing poems. It is useful to write verse of a frivolous, or deliberately unpoetic kind—to see, for example, if you can turn a newspaper article into rhymed stress-verse, to see if you can write lines in which there is a given rhyme pattern, simply out of ingenuity. One might, for example, choose to develop a progression of rhyming sounds, as in the following lines.

> The giant climbed the mountain track:
> (I read the story in a book)
> and found a salmon in a beck,
> and caught it with a silver hook.

Line A is in consonance with lines B, C, and D. Line B pararhymes C and finds a masculine rhyme in line D. Repeat the formula, altering the placing of the masculine rhyme for the sake of variety.

> He laughed to see the salmon leap
> and eagerly he raised it up.
> He gave its head a little tap,
> (He was a hungry sort of chap)

This is trivial, but it leads one to become familiar with the many ways in which words can be rhymed. One can also create rhyming lists in which each word is linked to its predecessor by some rhyming device or other, for example

Bat/mat/met/wet/wend/and/band/bind/sign/wine/won/

One can even construct a set of rhyme words and see if it is possible to, as it were, back a poem into it. One example might involve a selection of rhyming words all capable of dealing with a given subject. Such rhyme games, it must be emphasized, do far more than teach rhyme. They teach rhythm also, and many other aspects of word arrangement. Rhyme games have been known to result in poems. But, no matter how clever one may become at rhyming, or in writing proportional verse and stress verse, one has also to learn how to find oneself, not merely appropriate images, but an appropriate diction. Diction is the next aspect of poetry that we must tackle.

FOUR The Voices of Poetry

When one begins writing poetry one tends to use a language that convinces one that it is truly poetry that is being written. One uses a special voice, and the result is that the work is filled with adjectives and nouns that have been borrowed from poetry of the past. Poeticisms abound, and the imagery is more familiar than convincing. Ordinary word order is replaced by sentences to which poetic inversion is supposed to give dignity and force. Attitudes are conventional. Lovers contemplate the moon, and are filled with longing and solitude. 'What is life?' is the question on everyone's lips, and the answer usually involves the soul's sadness and the remoteness of God.

Much of this is understandable, especially if the writer is young, for many people are under the psychological necessity of dignifying their frustrations and loneliness by pretending to a degree of sensibility which makes them unique. *Il faut souffrir pour l'art*, said Flaubert. One might add that art is necessary to suffering, for the introspective, emotionally upset person will gravitate to the writing of poetry as naturally as a duck will take to water, though with considerably less elegance. One might, however, take the duck analogy further. A new-born duckling will, as Konrad Lorenz has pointed out, follow and accept as its mother the first live moving thing that it sees. In most cases this is its mother; in some cases it is not. The emotionally upset adolescent or middle-aged woman will follow poetry because it is the only immediately available mode of expressing, exploiting, and dignifying emotional disturbance. The spectacle is often both absurd and bewildering. It is bewildering because if one attempts to introduce these people to the writing of poetry proper, they frequently resist it. Poetry, to them, is an emotional security, and its strength lies in its familiarity, not in its novelty. Moreover, if one suggests that the right approach to writing, and to the self-discovery which is involved in becoming a writer, lies through the thorough investigation of one's own inner resources, such people are always inclined to say *Yes* and do otherwise.

In such situations there are two routes to follow. The first is to oblige such people to do the exercise outlined at the beginning of Chapter One. If they do, in fact, write for twenty minutes every night before going to bed, they usually find their problems become clearer to them, and less romantic. Also, they find that they are tottering on the brink of a kind of self-recognition which they must decide whether or not to accept. Acceptance leads, frequently, to abandonment of literary pre-tension. Sometimes, however, the person discovers that true poetry, exploratory poetry, is a solution, and there is a transformation of neurotic into poetic self-dramatization. If this transformation occurs, it may well lead to the creation of real poetry. After all, there is one theory which suggests that a great deal of literature derives from such a manœuvre. We dramatize ourselves in literature in order to compensate ourselves for our undramatic lives; we make our neuroses heroic by transforming them into poetic perceptions. There is a case of one student I knew who was writing pseudo-Wordsworthian poems, and who had a speech im-pediment. He undertook to write the nightly exercise for me. At the end of ten days he produced something closely resembling a real poem, written in ordinary day-to-day speech. So far as I know he never wrote another poem, but shortly afterwards, his speech impediment cleared up and he got married. This is an extreme case, admittedly, but it points to the close connection between the evasiveness of using outmoded poeti-cisms and the refusal to face one's own actual character and situation.

This may seem a long way around to discussing diction, but in fact the route I have taken is fairly direct. The second method of dealing with the young romanticist is to say, 'Do you, yourself, actually talk like this ordinarily? If not, does anybody? Can you even invent a character who would normally talk like this?' The answer is usually 'No' on all counts. An intelligent student will then ask why poetry should be in—to quote Wordsworth—'a selection of the language really used by men'. The answer to this is simple. In order to assent to the message of a poem, one has to believe in the speaker. Unless the writer is extraordinarily gifted, the reader will not find high poeticism credible. And it is high poeticism at which most of these would-be poets are aiming. It is not, however, the high-serious tone itself that I am perturbed about, it is its inappropriateness. The art of finding the appropriate diction is the art of adjusting the implied personality of the speaker to the nature of his vision, or vice versa.

There is a principle which I have previously described as that of Expectancy. This means that whenever we hear or read a small group of words, we intuit the nature of the words that are to follow. We make quick and perhaps superficial social judgements. Thus, if we hear a voice saying, 'Oh my beloved, moon of my delight', we are disturbed and perhaps amused by the incongruity if the voice continues by saying, 'let's have a cup of tea'. Similarly, if we hear a voice saying, elaborately, 'However subtle the philosophic distinction he makes, and however penetrating his solicitude for the terms of his own discourse, the fact indubitably remains that he is a poor slob!', we are startled by the phrase, *a poor slob*, because the words appear to belong to an educational level different from that of the preceding words. Much comic verse makes use of this expectancy principle. Lewis Carroll provides an example:

> The sun was shining on the sea,
> Shining with all his might
> He did his very best to make
> The billows smooth and bright—

'Ah,' we say, 'a romantic ballad'. Then we hear

> And this was odd

and we say, 'That's not the kind of critical statement the speaker of a ballad makes. A ballad speaker never comments in this way!' And we go on to read

> because it was
> The middle of the night

Odd now seems something of an understatement, and the linguistic shock that has been administered is clearly part of the writer's intention.

Diction expectancy resides partly in our judgement of the social and educational standing of the speaker, but also partly in our judgement of what is appropriate to a particular literary genre. Thus Rupert Brooke deliberately upset his readers by composing a sonnet which began in language that most readers would feel inappropriate to so meditative and traditional a form.

> The damned ship lurched and slithered. Quiet and quick
> My cold gorge rose; the long sea rolled; I knew
> I must think hard of something or be sick;
> And could think hard of only one thing—*you!*
> *A Channel Passage*

We judge, indeed, the appropriateness of diction in several ways, but mostly in accordance with rather simple general notions of literary and conversational norms.

Having said this, we must try to decide on the main norms—or so-called norms—in which we believe. It is not necessary for our beliefs to be sensible; they must only be those that are prevalent. Thus if we come across a four-letter word, a coarse obscenity, in a piece of writing we tend to think the speaker uneducated, even though we may know that educated, even highly educated, people also use obscenities. I have known many who are more foul-mouthed than most of the slum-dwellers I have known in both Europe and America.

What are these norms in which we believe? Firstly, we believe that such words as *peccadillo, spontaneity, conviction*—polysyllabic words which are also inclined to be abstract—are appropriate to an educated speaker, perhaps a pedagogue. We suspect him of being something of a spectator, rather than an active man, and are inclined to feel he may be unemotional. He is one of those who judges rather than feels.

On the other hand, if we read words like *shovel, bucket, tough, clay*, we suspect the speaker to be rather a downright character. He sees life as it is; he knows the ordinary realities. He does not protect himself by elaborate language. He speaks to the point.

We may, of course, find our initial judgements are altered by events, for no credible speaker talks with absolute consistency, and different aspects of a man's character may emerge at different times. Let us look at some passages of verse which show us types of both consistent and mixed diction.

Let us consider first the different variations of colloquial diction.

> Mr. Heath-Stubbs as you must understand
> Came of a gentleman's family out of Staffordshire
> Of as good blood as any in England
> But he was wall-eyed and his legs too spare.
>
> His elbows and finger joints could bend more ways than one
> And in frosty weather would creak audibly
> As to delight his friends he would give demonstration
> Which he might have done in public for a small fee . . .

These opening lines of John Heath-Stubbs's *Epitaph* are couched in colloquial diction, and include such commonplace locutions as *as you must understand, of as good blood as any*, and *for a small fee*. These near-clichés suggest that the speaker is not emotionally involved in what he is saying, and is playing it cool. The apparent carelessness of the rhythm reinforces this impression, while the slightly old-fashioned air of *came of a gentleman's family* and the touch of formality in the word order of *as to delight his friends he would* reinforce this impression of sophistication and good-breeding, while the objective, ironical tone is maintained by using the down-to-earth expression, *wall-eyed*. We are amused and entertained by what is, fairly obviously, a pose of ironic self-examination, and we can easily see how the tone is appropriate to the intent of the poem.

Another colloquial poem is Charlotte Mew's *The Farmer's Bride*, which is written in near-dialect.

> Three Summers since I chose a maid,
> Too young maybe—but more's to do
> At harvest-time than bide and woo.
>   When us was wed she turned afraid
> of love and me and all things human;
> Like the shut of a winter's day,
> Her smile went out, and 'twasn't a woman—
>   More like a little frightened fay.
>   One night, in the Fall, she runned away.

This is consistently simple diction, and the dialect usages force us to regard the speaker as a fairly simple-minded man. The diction itself suggests the kind of conflict the poem is to present, for the speaker of these lines could not be expected to understand the nature of a nervous breakdown. Thus the conflict between the tone of the voice and the content of the message provides a dramatic tension which makes the poem interesting.

Every poem is a dramatic monologue in which the character of the speaker is a part of the poem's message. Sometimes it is the major part of the poem's message as, perhaps, in Robert Browning's *My Last Duchess*, or T. S. Eliot's *The Love Song of J. Alfred Prufrock*. Most frequently, however, it is only one of many aspects of the poem. Here is the opening of a dramatic monologue by Wilfred Gibson.

> I hated him . . . his beard was red . . .
> Red fox, red thief! . . . Ah, God, that she—
> She with the proud and lifted head
> That never stooped to glance at me—
> So fair and fancy-free, should wed
> A slinking dog-fox such as he!
>
> *Red Fox*

Here, it is the organization rather than the vocabulary of the diction that is important. The broken-up sentences suggest that the speaker is thinking aloud, and that he is too emotional to arrange his words with precision or economy. The repetitions produce an effect of obsessiveness, also. It is clear that we here have an emotionally disturbed individual obsessed with the way the girl ignores him. He is, indeed, so disturbed that we want to know what is going to happen; we are even rather afraid that his hatred of the foxy man may lead to violence.

In all these cases the diction has been given its character by being limited. The vocabulary is a selected one, and the syntax has been consistent. In the vast majority of poems, however, the diction is less limited and therefore much more difficult to label. Take the opening lines of Phoebe Hesketh's poem, *The Fox*.

> It was twenty years ago I saw the fox
> Gliding along the edge of prickling corn,
> A nefarious shadow
> Between the emerald field and bristling hedge,
> On velvet feet he went.

Here the diction persuades us of the speaker having, not a particular, but a general and representative character. The direct colloquialism of *It was twenty years ago* is followed by the rather intellectual word *nefarious*. The sensuality of the speaker is clear, for the tactile is present in *prickling* and the visual in *emerald*. This last word is vivid and suggests that the speaker sees life dramatically, with intensity. We have in fact, an intelligent, sensitive, sensual, speaker with a feeling for drama and a capacity to look beneath the surface of events. The diction has, as it were, provided the credentials necessary to our believing the story.

Most poetry does this. It begins by proving to us that the speaker is reliable, and possessed of all his faculties. Occasionally, however, it is important to indicate that the speaker is in a condition of unusually heightened awareness. It is then that we get extreme diction of one kind or another. Consider, for example, the opening lines of Edith Sitwell's *Still Falls the Rain*.

> Still falls the Rain—
> Dark as the world of man, black as our loss—
> Blind as the nineteen hundred and forty nails
> Upon the Cross.

The opening inversion suggests a formal and dignified approach to the subject. The repetition of the formula *X as Y* gives an incantatory effect. The references are to huge concepts—*the world of man* and *the Cross*. The poem does not question, it asserts. And it asserts something totally unprovable. The assertive tone, combined with incantatory effects, usually convinces the reader that he is sharing the results of heightened sensibility, even of mystical vision.

> Never until the mankind making
> Bird beast and flower
> Fathering and all humbling darkness
> Tells with silence the last light breaking
> And the still hour
> is come of the sea tumbling in harness
>
> And I must enter again the round
> Zion of the water bead
> And the synagogue of the ear of corn . . .

This opening of Dylan Thomas's *A Refusal to Mourn* is also assertive and incantatory. It is, also, highly sensual and filled with references to great events.

Diction of this kind is not individuating; it does not create a particular, but a general speaker, but it makes us accept that speaker as an authority, even perhaps, as a seer. We have made one kind of social judgement. Sometimes we make a judgement in terms of genre. Consider the opening of Goldsmith's *Elegy on the Death of a Mad Dog*.

> Good people all, of every sort
> Give ear unto my song,

This establishes itself as folk-poetry, as a kind of ballad, immediately, by its tone and its rhythm. As we continue we find, of course, that Goldsmith has led us up the garden path, for the conventional introduction to a tale of love or heroism leads to something quite different, and the first verse clearly indicates the joke with its bathos:

> And if you find it wond'rous short
> It cannot hold you long.

The frustration of genre judgements is one of the diction techniques that is most frequently used. When Shakespeare began his sonnet with the phrase *My mistress' eyes* he made his readers expect a normal compliment, but he astonished them by continuing to say

> ... are nothing like the sun

Similarly Louis Simpson begins his poem, *The Green Shepherd*, with pastoral statements that lead us to expect simple sentiment, delicate imagery, and graceful eroticism. The second stanza, however, shifts its diction a little. Though we have the elegance of an inversion in the third line, the last line uses the direct and bathetic phrase *on her head* to suggest absurdity. The third stanza gives the game away entirely. The tone is now colloquial, with a touch of urbane sophistication in the phrase *certain reasons*. We have now got, it seems, a speaker who is surveying the traditional pastoral-heroic situation with a cool and sardonic eye. We are going to be entertained and disturbed by the contrast between the simplicity of the story and the sophistication of the narrator.

> Here sit a shepherd and a shepherdess,
> He playing on his melancholy flute;
> The sea wind ruffles up her simple dress
> And shows the delicacy of her foot.
>
> And there you see Constantinople's wall
> With arrows and Greek fire, molten lead;
> Down from a turret seven virgins fall,
> Hands folded, each one praying on her head.
>
> The shepherd yawns and puts his flute away.
> It's time, she murmurs, we were going back.
> He offers certain reasons she should stay—
> But neither sees the dragon on their tracks ...

Frustrating expectancy is one of the most frequent devices to make a poem interesting, and the opposing of tone to content is another. This last can reach extreme conditions when we arrive at the mock-heroic method where, in contrast to Simpson's poem, it is the subject matter which is commonplace and the voice which is artificial and traditional. Thomas Gray's portrait of the situation at the opening of his poem *On a Favourite Cat, drowned in a tub of Goldfishes* is a good example of the mock-heroic.

> 'Twas on a lofty vase's side
> Where China's gayest art had dyed
> The azure flowers that blow;
> Demurest of the tabby kind,
> The pensive Selima reclined,
> Gazed on the lake below.

This type of inflation need not be used entirely for comedy, however. Contrast between tone and content need not lead to the sardonicism of Simpson or the burlesque of Gray. It can lead in other directions.

All this, so far, has been from the reader's point of view. It is, however, the reader's point of view that emerges whenever we look at the first drafts of our poems and attempt to revise them. We must, in revising, pay attention to the appropriateness of our diction. Consider for example the following rough draft:

> Her eyes were of a blue serene,
> her hair was sheened with gold;
> she walked the velvet verdant green
> as did the queens of old.

This is old-fashioned, highly wrought stuff, making use of a deliberately high-romantic tone. The majority of the words are arranged to give a highly formal impression. There is a deliberate alteration of normal word order in *blue serene*—unless one accepts *serene* as a noun, in which case there is a deliberate sophistication of expression. I think we can make this more consistent in diction by taking out the commonplace words and putting in others. Let us rewrite it as:

> Her eyes were of a blue serene,
> her tresses sheened with gold;
> she trod the verdant velvet lane
> as did the queens of old.

Trod is less commonplace than *walked*, but it has a thumping sound and perhaps won't do. One could accept *That captain trod the deck* in a poem of this kind, but the lady is more delicate. She doesn't walk, or tread. Perhaps *she paced* would do ? Or *she glided*. This last spoils the tune, makes her stumble. Maybe if we alter it all into the historic present we can

3+

get away with *glides* and simultaneously make the shift into the more remote past of *as did the queens* more effective.

> Her eyes are of a blue serene,
> her tresses sheened with gold;
> she glides the velvet verdant lane
> as did the queens of old.

Did is, however, a rather coarse obvious word. Can one do better? *She glides . . . as glided . . .* No! Perhaps if we forget about the vocabulary of the diction and think of the dignity of its movement, we may solve the problem. Can we make it more formal by a parallelism?

> Her eyes are of a blue serene,
> her tresses sheened with gold;
> she walks the velvet verdant lane
> as walked the queens of old.

Walked is still wrong. *Wends*? Suitably archaic, certainly.

> She wends the velvet verdant lane
> as wended

No! Why not:

> as graceful queens of old?

Graceful is not archaic enough. And what about the alliteration in line three? Can't we repeat that effect?

> Her eyes are of a blue serene,
> her tresses sheened with gold;
> she wends the velvet verdant lane
> as queens were wont of old.

Not consonance, but assonance solves the problem. We now have a more or less authentic fake reproduction of an outmoded style.

Such a trivial problem may take hours of work, but the importance of solving it can hardly be overestimated. Diction problems are problems of the total attitude of the poem. It is interesting to look at a number of different translations of one poem to see just how versions, saying precisely the same thing, may differ in their diction, and therefore in their effect. Here are three modern versions of the opening of Homer's

Odyssey. The first is a prose translation by E. V. Rieu, and the two verse translations are by Albert Cook and Robert Fitzgerald respectively.

I. The hero of the tale which I beg the Muse to help me tell is that resourceful man who roamed the wide world after he had sacked the holy citadel of Troy. He saw the cities of many peoples and he learnt their ways. He suffered many hardships on the high seas in his struggles to preserve his life and bring his comrades home. But he failed to save those comrades, in spite of all his efforts. It was their own sin that brought them to their doom, for in their folly they devoured the oxen of Hyperion the Sun, and the god saw to it that they should never return. This is the tale I pray the divine Muse to unfold to us. Begin it, goddess, at whatever point you will.

II. Tell me, Muse, about the man of many turns, who many
    Ways wandered when he had sacked Troy's holy citadel;
    He saw the cities of many men, and he knew their thought;
    On the ocean he suffered many pains within his heart,
    Striving for his life and his companions' return.
    But he did not save his companions, though he wanted to:
    They lost their own lives because of their recklessness.
    The fools, they devoured the cattle of Hyperion,
    The Sun, and he took away the day of their return.
    Begin the tale somewhere for us also, goddess, daughter of Zeus.

III. Sing in me, Muse, and through me tell the story
    of that man skilled in all ways of contending,
    the wanderer, harried for years on end,
    after he plundered the stronghold
    on the proud height of Troy.
               He saw the townlands
    and learned the minds of many distant men,
    and weathered many bitter nights and days
    in his deep heart at sea, while he fought only
    to save his life, to bring his shipmates home.
    But not by will nor valor could he save them,
    for their own recklessness destroyed them all—
    children and fools, they killed and feasted on
    the cattle of Lord Hêlios, the Sun,
    and he who moves all day through heaven
    took from their eyes the dawn of their return.

    Of these adventures, Muse, daughter of Zeus,
    tell us in our time, lift the great song again.

The first version is written in straightforward English, and it seems, therefore, a straightforward tale, until we get to the last two sentences, where the speaker beseeches the Muse to help him. This is an attitude and a belief that the diction cannot encompass. It sounds artificial, and uneasy. If one is addressing a goddess, surely one uses a special tone of voice? The off-hand *Begin it, goddess, at whatever point you will* does not convince us of the respect in which the speaker must hold the goddess if he believes, as he states, that She is capable of inspiring him. The tone throughout is level, even flat, and its vocabulary is not such as to suggest that the Goddess is likely to listen. One might make the point that the inspiration the man asks for is clearly needed, and that therefore the flat tone is dramatically correct, but this does not seem an adequate excuse.

The second version has a slightly more vivid vocabulary, but it sometimes strays away from the ordinary without achieving heightened speech. *Man of many turns* seems unusual without being interesting. The inversion *Who many ways wandered* has a certain alliterative force and the word order adds a touch of formality appropriate to the occasion. This formality, however, is lost when we get to *suffered many pains within his heart* which lacks urgency as well as dignity, and when we get to . . . *he did not save his companions, though he wanted to* we have a colloquial dullness that is not appropriate to the telling of a heroic story. *Begin the tale somewhere* suggests lack of interest, for it hints at the question 'Where?' and the tone suggests the answer would be, 'Oh, any old where!'

The third version begins with high seriousness, and the vocabulary is less plain. The *resourceful man*, the *man of many turns* is now *that man skilled in all ways of contending*. The language is at once more precise and more elaborate. The word *contending* is a little less commonplace than the word *resourceful* and adds more to our understanding of the hero's character. *Roamed the wide world* (where *the wide world* is perilously close to a cliché), and *Who many ways wandered* (where we have a certain vagueness), are now replaced by *harried for years on end*, which is again more vigorous and informative. The first version told us that he *sacked the holy citadel of Troy*. Now, this does not suggest much save blasphemy. A holy place is not necessarily difficult of access. It adds little to our appreciation of the drama of the situation. The third version expands the story somewhat, but gives us both the difficulty of the manœuvre and the reason for making it, and substitutes for the concept *holy* that of *pride*, saying that he *plundered the stronghold on the proud heights of Troy*.

The test passage, is, however, the invitation to the Muse. Here

Fitzgerald easily wins the contest. He uses formal inversion again, thus indicating that special tone which implies respect, and he expands the notion to give us an idea of why inspiration is required. It is required because it is a *great song*. In another place too we find the earlier versions failing and Fitzgerald winning. Rieu makes his statement *the god saw to it that they should never return* both colloquial and abstract; the gods sound like businessmen or schoolteachers. Cook's gods are less commonplace; the sun god *took away the day of their return*. The snag with this is that it is a locution which is unfamiliar without being illuminating. The day of their return, it seems, existed, but was, somehow stolen. How can a day be stolen, even by the sun god? There is an obvious answer, but we should not have felt like pausing to ask the question. Fitzgerald explains it more clearly. The sun god *took from their eyes the dawn of their return*; he thus affected the men, rather than the day itself, and we can explain the statement in terms of either blindness or death. There remains a question in our mind, but it is one that we confidently expect to be answered by the poem itself. We want to know *how* it happened— was it blindness, or death, or (perhaps) they did return, but in darkness. We don't ask, 'What does the poet mean?' We ask, 'How did it happen?'

Now, these three passages differ from one another in more than diction, of course. We are not concerned with accuracy of translation here, however. We are concerned with whether the diction is such as it can support the attitudes it expresses. Fitzgerald's version does; the others do not. And yet, let us notice, Fitzgerald has not, in his efforts towards high epic seriousness, become outlandish. He has become sophisticated, and perhaps more leisurely, but, again, one must remember that leisure-liness also implies an attitude towards one's subject matter. If one spends ten lines saying something it suggests one believes that the subject is important; if one takes two lines it suggests that one does not feel the subject deserves much attention. This is, of course, only the case if the leisureliness does not result in tedious prolixity. In general, however, the heroic story, the epic, demands leisurely progress, for it demands that we pay reverence to every ascertainable detail of such an important story. 'Brevity', it has been said, 'is the soul of wit'. Let us look at a number of translations of quite a different kind of poem, an epigram by Palladas, the fifth-century Alexandrian poet.[1] Andrew Sinclair translated it as:

[1] Πᾶσα γυνὴ χόλος ἐστίν. ἔχει δ᾿ ἀμαθὰς δύω ὥρας,
  τὴν μίαν ἐν θαλαμῳ, τὴν μίαν ἐν θανάτῳ.
(Greek Anthology Book IV, Loeb Classical Library, Book XI, Epigram 381).

> Every woman is annoying,
> Yet twice she's ripe and red:
> The first time when she's marrying,
> The second when she's dead.

This is neatly rhymed, but the vocabulary seems odd. The phrase *ripe and red* has unfortunate secondary associations. The irreverent reader is liable to see a woman the colour of a beetroot. One assumes Sinclair is thinking of a ripe apple, but this comparison is not in the poem itself. And, in spite of our willingness to believe the speaker is talking fantastically, it is hard to see that a woman may be *ripe and red* when she is dead. *Rotten* perhaps, and *white* possibly. Let us look at Louis Untermeyer's version.

> No man regards his wife with pleasure, save
> Twice: in her bridal bed, and in her grave.

This is neat, but the rove-over[2] gives the word *Twice* a thunderous emphasis, and the pause after it has to be so long that it is hard to read the sentence smoothly. On the other hand the diction is consistent. It is the language of ordinary conversation slightly qualified by the use of the word *save* which is a little artificial. The word *regards* and the phrase *bridal bed* are also a little more formal than the usual conversation, however, so that the whole epigram is reasonably consistent in tone. Only that awkward rove-over prevents the urbanity from total success.

R. A. Furness's version is also neat, and a little more colloquial.

> A woman's a pest,
> but is twice at her best:
> The first time, in bed;
> And the second time, dead.

This poem opens with slangy directness. If we accept the speaker as a brusque, downright, slangy sort of man, however, can we really accept his touch of long-windedness in repeating the word *time* when the repetition is unnecessary for the sense? I think we can. The repetition is that beloved of anecdotalists; it is there to delay the dénouement and make the last word more of a shock. My only quarrel is with the word *but*. In what way does the statement that a woman is *twice at her best* oppose the statement that she is *a pest* ? It is not quite a correct use of the *but*. I could, however, accept this, if it were not that if a woman is a pest, then at her *best* she should surely be even more pestilential than usual ? There are difficulties here, but not as many as in Willis Barnstone's version.

> A woman will gnaw at your bile
> Yet she has two fine seasons:
>   one, in her bridal bed;
>   two, when she is dead.

Apart from the distracting unpleasantness of the first line (could one in any case gnaw bile ? Isn't bile fluid ?), this poem has an unbalanced diction. The opening two lines are confusing. If a woman is a creature that gnaws, then does she have *seasons* as years do, or vegetable growths ? Does she spend a *season* in her *bridal bed* ? Surely the bed is only *bridal* for a short time, and that is the point of the joke ? The word *seasons* is wrong. Moreover, the *gnaw at your bile* suggests a bitter, almost savage, speaker, while the remainder of the poem does not support this viewpoint, being quite coolly terse. The parallelism at the end of the version is clumsy because incomplete. The *in* should, ideally, be paralleled by an *in*, just as Andrew Sinclair paralleled his *when* and Untermeyer his *in*.

My own solution to the problem is to maximize the parallelism at the end of the verse, and to shift from a slightly artificial colloquialism in the first three lines to downright slang for the punch line.

> Woman is a dreadful creature
> and gives pleasure twice at most:
> once when she gives up her virtue,
> once when she gives up the ghost.

This is not perfect, either. *Gives up her virtue* is far too vague, but *virginity* is too long for the line and *hymen* too grossly clinical. I leave it to readers to find another solution.

It can be seen from these examinations of these two sets of translations that the diction of a poem can be the very heart of it. It is, in most cases, the diction that decides whether or not we find the whole thing credible, not as a truth, but as a statement by another human creature.

How can we make our own poems credible in diction? There are some exercises that can help. One is to construct a poem in dialogue form so that the distinction between the two voices is clearly noticeable. The first voice can be sophisticated, that of an educated person, and the second that of a naïve one. The tension thus set up often produces dramatic excitement and, as I suggested in Chapter Three, also provides something of a poetic plot. Another exercise is to attempt to change the diction of an existing poem without changing its general meaning.

This means, usually, that the scale has to be altered. If we attempted to rewrite the first stanza of Grey's *An Ode on a Favourite Cat drowned in a tub of Goldfishes* in commonplace colloquial language we would find ourselves having to do it with far fewer words, for prolixity and loving detail are characteristic of the heroic but not of the colloquial mode. We might end up, badly, with something like:

> A cat sat by the fishbowl's rim,
> and very thoughtfully stared in.
>
> With waving tail, complacent, she
> purred loudly at what she could see.

This is hardly poetry, but it gets the general picture adequately. What about heightening the language of a rather bald piece of verse, however? Let us maltreat the opening three lines of Robert Frost's *Acquainted with the Night*.

> I have been one acquainted with the night.
> I have walked out in rain—and back in rain.
> I have outwalked the furthest city light.

If we wish to heighten the language here, we must make it less summary. This means we must try to elaborate, and therefore perhaps interpret the poem.

> I have long been a familiar of the darkness,
> and have travelled far in the driving rain,
> only to return with the rain still falling;
> I have journeyed beyond the edge of the town,
> until behind me the last small light blinked, failing.

We might, however, if we were feeling perverse enough, choose to attack it differently.

> I have been a night walker,
> walking out in the rain,
> that poured like doom from the heavens,
> and walking back again.
>
> I have been a night walker,
> travelling beyond the town
> till the last small flicker of lamplight
> faltered and died down.

Or one might imitate the prolixity of Whitman:

> I have been one acquainted with the night, the dark patches
>   of roadways, the looming hedgerows, the night owl's cry.
> I have journeyed far in the falling rain to return with
>   the rain still falling
> I have crossed the city limits, beyond the very end of
>   the lights, beyond the outermost edge of the sleeping world.

This is no more than a game, perhaps, but it teaches dexterity and an eye for what is characteristic in diction.

Another exercise is to begin a poem with a line donated by somebody else, preferably unfamiliar. How would one, for example, continue a poem that began:

> Silently, slowly, darkly . . .

Or

> As I went out one morning

Or

> Was it the first word heard ?

Or

> Quiet, he said, Be quiet . . .

Or

> Never did nothing wrong,

Or

> Only the sound of the waves . . .?

In order to play this game at all one has to make a number of judgements as to the diction already partly established. *As I went out one morning* is so clearly a ballad line that one has no difficulty, but what about *Was it the first word heard?*

3*

> Was it the first word heard,
> Or the second, that hit me hard?
> Was it the 'no' or the 'never'
> That altered all I desired
> into a . . .

Or, perhaps

> Was it the first word heard
> in Eden? I half believe
> when Adam woke from his slumber
> and turned to sleeping Eve,
>
> he murmured it, unknowing
> even what words might be.
> Or was it the last word spoken
> as from the forbidden tree
>
> the hand reached down the apple
> and the serpent grinned above,
> or the first word of their exile?
> And did it sound like Love?

This version requires attention. If the man half believes something in stanza one, he is unlikely to say, doubtfully, *Or was it* in stanza two. There must be more of a dramatic shift in viewpoint. Let us rewrite:

> Yet it could be the last word spoken

But if we know the word, as we must in order to talk about it at all, the last line is absurd. We must revise again:

> the hand reached down the apple,
> and the serpent grinned above,
> or the first word of their exile?
> And was it, truly, Love?

Perhaps,

> It was all three, and Love.

Bad poetry emerges easily from such exercises, but in doing them one becomes familiar with problems of diction, and learns that the voice of the poem is a most important part of its meaning.

Most young poets, of course, ask, 'How can I find my own voice?' They feel that they must achieve a highly personal and idiosyncratic style. They are aware that one can tell a poem of John Donne, or Alexander Pope, or William Blake, or Browning, or T. S. Eliot, or Dylan Thomas, or e. e. cummings from all others simply by observing the diction and movement. The highly personal style is also, however, the consequence of a slow development of speech characteristics appropriate to the particular poet's main concerns and obsession. It cannot be faked or invented; it has to grow. One can perhaps accelerate the process by taking a particular technical device and exploiting it to the exclusion of all others, and become known as the master of a particular form, or genre, or mood. Thus, we can say that Ogden Nash became the master of the couplet of unequal length and the complex bathetic rhyme. We can point to lesser writers, and maintain that Coventry Patmore made himself the master, for his period, of the poem dealing with domesticity, and that A. E. Housman became the laureate of youthful mortality and faithless love. We find, however, if we do this that we are making statements about themes as well as diction, and about prosody also. The three are so connected as to be inseparable. Indeed, as it is often the movement of speech that gives it a great deal of its character, we must now turn from considering diction to discussing prosody.

FIVE The Rhythms of Poetry

The study of English Prosody has been bedevilled by many false assumptions. The first, made by those writers and critics educated in the classics, was that it was possible to treat English metres as if they were Greek or Latin ones. The second was that there were rules which were inviolable and that one was allowed, for example, only one variant foot in any given line of verse, and that it was a sin to include too many hypercatalectic or catalectic [1] lines in one piece of poetry. Although we must look at the conventional academic approach to metre (for it has its uses) it is best to start off very simply indeed and consider exactly what we mean by Prosody, and of what the rhythm of poetry consists.

Firstly, it is clear that we must be pragmatic. A line of verse must be capable of being spoken aloud with ease and in such a manner that the speaker remains a credible human being. The only exceptions to this rule are those poems which are written for the eye and an even smaller number which use the distortion of normal accent and rhythm for special effects. If we scan a poem in terms of heavily stressed syllables, and unstressed syllables only, we are going to produce only a rough approximation to the facts. Consider the opening stanza of a poem that has been commonly regarded as the most perfect example of the use of iambic pentameter in English. Let us underline those syllables which should be stressed if this stanza is, in fact, as perfect as it is reputed to be.

> The curfew tolls the knell of parting day,
> The lowing herd wind slowly o'er the lea,
> The plowman homeward plods his weary way,
> And leaves the world to darkness and to me.

This is, surely, ridiculous. Firstly we notice that the word *wind* is far too important for us not to give it more stress than the other unstressed

[1] See page 157.

68

syllables in the line. In fact, surely it gets as much stress as the syllable *low*. We can either agree to give it a heavy stress or what is called a secondary stress, which is to say a degree of stress halfway between full stress and none. As for the last line, who, speaking normally, would stress *and*? It is clearly unstressed.

This last line, however, presents another problem. If we read it with any sensitivity, surely we pause before the word *and*, partly to give the statement a little more interest rhythmically, and partly because *and to me* is tagged on to the earlier statements, almost as an afterthought. If we read it levelly we appear to equate the significance and importance of *darkness* with the significance and importance of *me*, and thus pervert the tone and intent of a poem in which the role of the speaker is most carefully underplayed. We must, in fact, realize that pauses have to be considered as part of the rhythmic scheme and, perhaps, indicate the pause by a /, thus:

> And leaves the world to darkness / and to me.

This particular poem does not use dramatic pauses very much, so we don't have to consider whether we should indicate the length of the pause by using such notations as / or // or ///. Other poems will, however, present us with this problem.

The effect of a pause in a line of regular verse is also to alter the speed with which the adjacent words are spoken. Gray's stanza moves slowly and leisurely, and, to my ear, hardly changes speed at all, until that pause in the last line. Then, however, as if to compensate for the pause, it does speed up and the *and to* is, or appears to be, spoken more quickly. Thus we may find ourselves wishing to indicate alterations of speed in the poems we look at. How about doing it like this?

> And leaves the world to darkness / and to me.

Gray's poem is, as I say, very level in tone. If we are to get any further with seeing what characterizes verse rhythm we need to take an additional example. Let us, again, take a familiar verse. Here is the opening stanza of Keat's *Ode to Autumn*. Let us read it aloud and notice first where we naturally place the stresses.

> Season of mists and mellow fruitfulness!
> Close bosom-friend of the maturing sun;
> Conspiring with him how to load and bless
> With fruit the vines that round the thatch-eaves run;

This is obviously inadequate. Firstly, we have to say *Close bosom-friend* more slowly than we said *fruitfulness*, because *fruitfulness* ends with two unstressed syllables and the major part of the meaning is in the first syllable so we can take the other two syllables easy. But the unstressed syllable of *bosom* is essential to the sense, so it gets a minute degree more attention than the *-fulness* in *fruitfulness*. Here we can recognize that the rhythm of the poem is in part dependent upon our giving proper attention, when we speak, to the syllables essential to the meaning. We may not stress them, but we must not glide over them. Another factor of rhythm has emerged. But let us look at the third line. We don't surely glide over each of the words *with*, *him*, *how*, and *to* at the same rate, and yet we can't over-stress either the word *him* or the word *how* or we would be emphasizing either the importance of the personality of the sun, or the mode and difficulty of the process of loading and blessing. My own solution is not to stress any word heavily but to pause very briefly between *him* and *how*, so as to indicate the structure of the statement and avoid a mid-line gallop that would be inappropriate to the mood. The words before and after a pause always get a little more attention than others. There is time to recall what one has just heard and to prepare for what one is about to hear, so even if the words remain unstressed and rapidly spoken they are more clearly heard than some others. The middle of this line does move quickly, however. I think I'd scan it as:

$$\text{Conspi}\underset{\_}{\text{r}}\text{ing with h}\overset{+}{\text{i}}\text{m} \; / \; \text{how t}\overset{+}{\text{o}} \underset{\_}{\text{load}} \text{ and } \underset{\_}{\text{bless}}$$

There is a rove-over at the end of this line, so that the pause between *bless* and *with* is smaller than that between *fruitfulness* and *close*. The last line, however, surely moves more slowly, than the others, for more of the words require us to dwell upon them. We need to be able to indicate this also. We are rapidly approaching a situation where something like a musical notation is required.

This, of course, has been the solution of several prosodists. A pseudo-musical notation enables them not only to indicate the degree of stress, the altering speed, and the varying length of pause, with some precision, but also enables them to indicate changes in pitch. Pitch changes are important, as, of course, are all the phonetic aspects of verse. In the Keats lines for example we drop our voice on the word *sun*. I suspect, too, that we lighten our tone a little as we read *With vines the eaves that round the* and then lower the pitch gradually thereafter.

I am not concerned, here and now, to provide a musical notation for these or any lines. I am only concerned to point out all the elements that go to make up verse rhythm. We have seen, so far, that we must consider degrees of stress (full, half, none, are the three obvious ones), degrees of pause, alterations of speed, and alterations of pitch. This last becomes most important in dramatic verse. Look at the opening of Robert Browning's *Bishop Blougram's Apology*.

> No more wine ? then we'll push back chairs and talk.
> A final glass for me, though: cool, i'faith!

Here even the most rudimentary reading demands that we recognize, not only a manner of speech, but an actual human situation. On *wine* the voice rises in interrogation. There is a pause for the speaker's companion to shake his head or nod. The line then speeds up, for the following words are casual, unforced, even perhaps a little slurred. The pause between *wine* and *then* is certainly shorter than that between *though* and *cool* where, clearly, the speaker has paused to drink. The casual *i'faith* means it must be spoken on a lower pitch and more quickly than the word *cool*. The word *me* is, clearly emphasized and on a rising note, while *though* drops away as merely a meaningless conversational noise. We might, using our very simple method of notation scan it all as:

> No more wine ? // then we'll push back chairs and talk./
>
> A final glass for me, though: /// cool, i'faith.

This notation does not, however, recognize that there are several ways of saying *No more wine?* according to one's interpretation of the speaker's tone. *No more wine?* could mean that the listener might have more cheese, or coffee, or what-have-you. Emphasis might be on the word *more*, and suggest that the man had already had quite a lot. And so we could go on. In other words, no matter how precise one's notation may be, it is always the notation of a particular interpretation, and can never be the pattern of more than one rendering. If we take this to its logical conclusion we can see that most prosodic analysis, and most statements as to the regularity or otherwise of given lines are highly suspect. Each speaker is his own prosodist; each musician not only plays the score differently, but plays a different score.

Nevertheless, there is some point in going further into orthodox metres, for they provide us with useful tools for reworking our own poems. Many times a poet will write a verse which sounds perfect to his ear, but on attempting to write a second verse with the same rhythm he will find he can't do it. He cannot understand exactly what the tune is until he has at least partly analysed it. Frequently, too, one senses that a line sounds wrong, but can't tell why. If one analyses the poem, however, one often discovers that an irregularity of rhythm, or even a too regular use of rhythm, has resulted in a falsity of tone. It is not necessary for the poet to know all the names for all the metres discovered (and sometimes, I fear, invented) by the prosodists. Nevertheless, for those readers who find themselves entertained or stimulated by the practising of strict metrical exercises I have included more than enough of the information they need in an appendix.

No amount of study of metrical forms, however, can give a poet a good ear for verse. Indeed, an obsession with metrical regularity or metrical ingenuity may damage his work irreparably unless he has the good fortune to be an Alfred Tennyson rather than, let us say, a Lord Macaulay or an Austin Dobson. Such a concern can lead to dead rectitude, or to the production of self-indulgent exhibitions of mere dexterity. In general, poets first of all create their rhythmic patterns by ear and only later sometimes analyse what they have done in order to assist the business of revision. They may, however, in an attempt to learn from other writers how various effects have been achieved, analyse those poems that most interest them. Mostly, however, they are liable simply to read the poems aloud often enough to get the things into their head and then, mynah-bird-like, imitate until they feel they have got the trick of it. There are, however, some tricks that a poet needs to know, however intuitive his writing may be.

Firstly, the ear cannot tolerate the unvaried repetition of a simple rhythmic tune for more than three or four lines at a time. The longer the line the more tedious this repetitiveness becomes. Lines must be varied by catalexis, hypercatalexis,[1] and substitution. A certain *lameness* one might say, makes the speech humanely inexact. Robert Lowell has gone on record as saying that he often revises his poetry towards, rather than away from, metrical irregularity.

Secondly, in English verse the hexameter can only work for more than one line at a time if it is broken up by means of a quite emphatic pause. Most hexameters in English really consist of two lines, written as one. The heptameter almost invariably works out, in experience, as two lines of four and three feet each, especially when iambic or trochaic.

Thirdly, the shorter the line in rhymed verse, the more clangorous and emphatic does the rhyme appear to be. Only if one is attempting a

[1] See page 157.

Pope-like wit and clarity should one end couplets with a succession of full rhymes. Rhymes appear both self-conscious and over-cerebral when they force themselves upon one with undue emphasis. If one is not attempting deliberately witty verse, but wishes to rhyme, one should use near-rhymes more often than full ones in short-lined verse.

Fourthly, the effect of a succession of neatly alternating stressed and unstressed syllables is to make the line have a rocking motion, and become sing-song. This is especially true of dactyls and anapaests.[1] Such lines tend, because of this, to gain speed as the poem progresses. If one does not want to write headlong poetry one should obstruct the lines with pauses or with consonantal groupings that, being difficult to pronounce quickly, slow up the line and compel the reader to pay attention to what is going on.

Fifthly, the more regular one's metre the closer does the poem come to sounding like a song. The more irregular the metre the closer it will come to conversation. When we get conversational diction in emphatic metre we get doggerel. When we get impassioned and romantic statements in highly irregular metre we are sometimes slowed up so much that we give the romanticism a wholly inadvisable amount of close scrutiny. It is difficult to stomach some lyrical perceptions if one cannot, as it were, sing them.

Sixthly, if we attempt to use complex metres we must be sure that the metre is not grossly inappropriate to the subject matter. A small sad story about the death of a pet cat may be touching in trochaic trimeter and ridiculous in dactyllic hexameter.

Seventhly, the way to learn how to handle metre and rhythm is to continually listen to it in all its manifestations. Folk poetry, folk songs, and popular songs can teach one the easy, and perhaps superficial, handling of lyrical sentiment in conversational language. Let me try to give examples.

> The dark and lonely city fills the night
> with fears and bitter dreams of dying men
> enclosed in shabby rooms that only hear
> the sounds of breath and restless weary sheets
> and driving rain beyond the battered walls
> of blank despair that none can give them rest
> or ease the thumping heart with calming words.

This is blank verse (acatalectic unrhymed iambic pentameter), and it

[1] See page 156.

sounds both dull and automatic. Let us first of all indulge in a little obvious substitution.

> The dark and lonely city fills the night
> with fears and the bitter dreams of dying men,
> sounds of the restless breath, the weary sheets,
> and harsh rain whispering beyond the walls,
> and they despair that none will give them rest
> and ease the thundering heart with calming words.

We need more pauses, and more variation still.

> Lonely and dark, the city brings the night
> fear and the dying dreams of bitter men
> trapped in their shabby rooms. All they can hear
> is their own breath, the rustling of restless sheets,
> and harsh rain on the pane. The walls themselves
> are battered by despair. There is no hope.
> There's no one near to ease them with kind words.

It seems to me that this is prolix. Perhaps the line is too long, though, its being a rather gloomy passage, the long line has some advantages.

> Lonely and dark, the city night,
> a dream of bitter dying men
> in shabby rooms, exuding fear,
> hears nothing but its weary breath,
> and restless sheets, and driving rain
> upon smeared windows. Even walls
> are battered by despair it seems,
> and no voice offers hope or calm.

This is prosy. The rhythm moves too dully still. Perhaps if one were to knock it about still further ?

> Lonely and dark,
> the city fills with dreams
> of bitter dying men,
> in shabby rooms.
> They listen to their breathing,
> and to the scratch
> and rustle of their sheets,
> as driving rain
> rattles upon the window.
> Hopeless, blank,
> the battered walls exude despair.
> None comes.

This looks a lot freer, but is it?

> Lonely and dark, the city fills with dreams
> of bitter dying men in shabby rooms.
> They listen to their breathing, and the scratch
> and rustle of their sheets as driving rain
> rattles upon the window. Hopeless, blank
> the battered walls exude despair. None comes.

We have, in fact, returned to a freer blank verse, in which there is a good deal of substitution, and many of the lines have only four stresses. The passage still suffers, however, from every line ending automatically on a stressed syllable.

> Lonely and dark, the city fills with dreams
> of bitter dying men in shabby rooms.
> They listen to their own breathing and the rustle
> of their restless sheets as driving rain
> rattles upon the window. Blank and battered
> walls exude despair. No comfort comes.

This is better, but there seems still to be a few bugs in it. In lines 3 and 4 the repetition of that *the* sound seems a little excessive.

> Lonely, dark, the city fills with dreams
> of bitter dying men in shabby rooms.
> They listen to their breathing and the restless
> whispers of shifting sheets, while driving rain
> rattles at dirty windows. Blank and battered
> walls exude despair. No comfort comes.

Too many adjectives.

> Lonely and dark, the city fills with dreams
> of bitter dying men in shabby rooms.
> They listen to their breathing, to the whisper
> of the shifting sheets and to the rain
> driving at blank-eyed windows. Battered walls
> exude despair. No word of comfort comes.

At this point one might well choose to abandon the passage entirely, having come to the conclusion that the game is not worth the candle. This often happens. Usually, however, the theme recurs in a later poem or, some months afterwards, one finds the lines in a pile of manuscript and discovers that the game isn't quite lost, after all.

The amending of verse, the revision of it, has been called by Robert Graves *secondary composition*, and it has been said that it is the relative ability of young writers to revise their drafts that separates the men from the boys. It is certainly true that the ability totally to alter the rhythm and diction of a draft must come high upon the list of desirable skills.

Let us take another point. I have said that if one writes in a simple diction of simple matters it may prove advisable to give one's statements the form of a lyric rather than a passage of conversational verse, because we will accept simplicity, even naïveté, in a fairly smoothly moving song, while we may be forced to dwell upon it and question it if it is couched in irregular colloquial rhythms. Consider for example the following passage:

> When I was twenty-one, an old wise man
> Told me, 'Give away money, if you wish,
> But never lose your heart. Pearls, Diamonds, Rubies
> Can be discarded, but you must stay fancy-free.'
> I was twenty-one; He was wasting his breath.

This is prosy enough, colloquial enough, and in a form of irregular blank verse. To make it less dull one would have to heighten the vocabulary considerably, and thus alter the nature of the anecdote. How much better to turn it into a song . . .

> When I was one-and-twenty
>   I heard a wise man say,
> 'Give crowns and pounds and guineas
>   But not your heart away;
> Give pearls away and rubies,
>   But keep your fancy free.'
> But I was one and twenty
>   No use to talk to me.

A. E. Houseman

Housman's poem derives its persuasiveness from its lyric simplicity. It is not, however, a true song, though it has been set to music. True songs tend to be even thinner and simpler, unless they are patter-songs, or songs which must be rendered in a near-recitative, as are many blues.

The use of a given metre or poetic form is often dependent for its success upon the spacing of the pauses, as much as upon anything else.

After all, if one has a passage of metrical verse it can be sawn up into different lengths, and one soon discovers that in one case a long line may be more appropriate than a short one, and that in another the reverse may be true. Relineating poems, one's own and others', is a very valuable exercise. Let us consider relineating a passage of verse. Thomas Moore wrote, in a definite metre, and with full rhyming:

> I saw from the beach, when the morning was shining,
> A bark o'er the waters move gloriously on;
> I came, when the sun o'er that beach was declining,—
> The bark was still there, but the waters were gone!

Now, of these four lines, three divide easily into two halves. Let us therefore relineate the passage thus:

> I saw from the beach,
> when the morning was shining,
> A bark o'er the waters
> move gloriously on;
> I came, when the sun
> o'er that beach was declining,—
> The bark was still there,
> but the waters were gone!

What has happened? We have maximized the pauses that previously occurred in the middle of the lines. As a consequence the metre is now much more obvious, and the rocking motion of the verse has become too emphatic, at least to my ear. Moreover, what was previously an internal, and therefore partly disguised, rhyme, that of *on* with *sun* has now become prominent. Let us split it up in another, less immediately obvious, fashion.

> I saw from the
> beach when the
> morning was shining,
> a bark o'er the
> waters move
> gloriously on;
> I came when the
> sun o'er that
> beach was declining,—
> the bark was
> still there but the
> waters were gone.

This type of lineation is one involving what I would like to call syntactical suspense. It hurries the poem along by making as many lines as possible obviously incomplete statements. It makes the verse more exciting, perhaps, but the degree of suspense created is far greater than the subject matter can carry without a sense of anti-climax. The re-lineation does draw attention to the echoing usage of *the* and *that* and *there*, however. One might maximize this effect by relineating the last three lines again:

> the bark was still there
> but the
> waters were gone

It is clear that the placing of the sound *the* at the same point in the first, third, and fourth lines of the original version gives the poem a tight pattern. Do we wish, however, to reveal this, or to disguise it? What aspect of our verse form do we wish to be most immediately apparent to the reader? I myself feel that Moore's own version is the right one, but also feel that relineating it has taught us a good deal.

Sometimes relineation can affect the metrical effect much more seriously than in this particular case. Consider this passage by Swinburne. The first four lines of *Hesperia* read:

> Out of the golden remote wild west where the sea without shore is,
>   Full of the sunset, and sad, if at all, with the fulness of joy,
> As a wind sets in with the autumn that blows from the region
>   of stories,
>   Blows with a perfume of songs and of memories beloved from
>   a boy[1]

[1] These are dactyllic hexameters; The first line can/be scanned as:

$$/\text{xx} /\text{xx} // /\text{xx} /\text{xx} /\text{x}$$

The line is thus catalectic, with spondaic substitution in the third foot. The second line can be scanned as:

$$/\text{xx} /\text{xx} /\text{xx} /\text{xx} /\text{xx} /$$

This is catalectic dactyllic hexameter with no substitution.
The third line could be scanned as:

$$\text{xx} // /\text{xx} /\text{xx} /\text{xx} /\text{xx} /\text{x}$$

Here the first four is ionic (a minore). The fourth line could be read as:

$$/\text{xx} /\text{xx} /\text{xx} /\text{xxx} /\text{xx} /$$

If we read *memories* as *mem'ries*, then the line involves no substitution. If we sound all three syllables of this word, then we have a paean substituted in the fourth foot.

I said earlier that hexameters, in English, always broke down into shorter lines. Is this true here ?

> Out of the golden remote wild west
>   where the sea without shore is,
> Full of the sunset, and sad, if at all,
>   with the fulness of joy,
> As a wind sets in with the autumn
>   that blows from the region of stories,
> Blows with a perfume of songs,
>   and of memories beloved from a boy

It appears I am wrong, but the reason is worth examining. Firstly, Swinburne has made his hexameters in such a way that one cannot break them automatically always at the same point. He has done this by giving his original opening line a series of heavy stresses in the middle and then alliterating these syllables with the next unstressed syllable so that one naturally moves ahead easily. Change the *West* to *South* and the relineation becomes much more acceptable. In the second line of the original, he has thrown in the conversational, almost parenthetical, phrase *if at all*, thus speeding up the line, so that, again we move rapidly to the next word. We can see the difference if we replace *sad, if at all* with *sadly enthralled*. If we wrote *sadly endowed*, however, the *w* sound would carry us on more quickly, and the more quickly because it had been used before. The next two lines do divide easily, and almost automatically at the same point.

Swinburne, however good or bad he is as a poet, is an exceptional metrist. He usually solves the problem of hexameters by altering speed and pitch, by using interjections and parentheses, and by alliterative linkings. Later in *Hyperia*, however, the tendency is, deliberately, less controlled and one can easily relineate, thus:

> As the cross that a wild nun clasps
>   till the edge of it bruises her bosom,
> So love wounds as we grasp it,
>   and blackens and burns as a flame;
> I have loved overmuch in my life;
>   when the live bud bursts with the blossom
> Bitter as ashes or tears is the fruit,
>   and the wine thereof shame.

This metre is regular enough, and the poem is distinctly rhetorical.

79

It compels our assent by insisting upon its character as a near-song or chant. Were the metre less regular we would almost certainly be unable to accept the extremeness of the statements. This is again, a case of the special voice being used.

The special voice and the dactyllic metre are here appropriate to the nature of the poem. But sometimes we find poems which are comic because an inappropriate metre is being used. Consider the following lines:

> The kitten sat under the lilac in calm meditation;
> The sky was as blue as could be and the grass was so green
> that the kitten seemed poised on the edge of some primitive
>   vision,
> primeval, obscure, and remote as a jaguar's dream.

Here the calm of the meditation, and of the scene, and the profundity of the vision indicated are totally at variance with the skipping motion of the lines.

$$x/x \; //x \; x/x \; x/x \; x/x$$

$$x/x \; x/x \; x/x \; x/x \; x/$$

$$xx/x \; //x \; x/x \; x/x \; / \; x/x$$

$$//x \; x/x \; x/x \; x/x \; x/$$

I wrote a poem that began something like this one.

> The cat sat under the lilac.
> It was black,
> The grass was green, the sky blue,
> and it stood
> black under the lilac
> that was lilac
> under a sky that was all over blue. . . . .

This is at once simpler and slower. It is almost in kindergarten language. The rhythm sounds as naïve and unforced as the situation. I did not, in this poem, tackle the profundity of the cat's dream, however. Perhaps for that one would need another metre still.

> Under the tree, the cat,
> black in the green
> and blue of summer prowls
> some primitive dream,
> lithe and lean as a jaguar . . .

This does not have the heavy sombre quality required. Perhaps one should think of a freer form of verse.

> The cat sleeps under the lilac.
> Its fur shines.
> It kneads its paws on the dry roots,
> the withered grass,
> as if some primeval fury
> lay in its claws,
> and obscure destinies of the jaguar.

Once we attempt free verse, or *vers libre*, we are, of course leaving orthodox prosody behind. Or so we are told. And yet, the only difference between free verse and metrical verse is the nature of the recurring rhythmical units, and the use of the pause.

The earliest type of *vers libre* is what I have called Proportional Verse. Consider this passage from the Bible.

> Give unto the Lord, O ye mighty,
> give unto the Lord glory and strength.
> Give unto the Lord the glory due unto his name;
> worship the Lord in the beauty of holiness.
> The voice of the Lord is upon the waters:
> the God of glory thundereth:
> the Lord is upon many waters.
>
> (*Psalm XXIX*)

Now look at this passage from Walt Whitman.

> When I heard the learn'd astronomer,
> When the proofs, the figures, were ranged in columns before me,
> When I was shown the charts and diagrams, to add, divide, and
> measure them,
> When I sitting heard the astronomer where he lectured with much
> applause in the lecture room,
> How soon unaccountably I became tired and sick . . .

It is easy to separate these passages into small rhythmic groups. Frequently the groups have the same number of stresses. Sometimes they appear to be similar only, however, in their duration, or, perhaps, in their being composed in a limited number of formulae. We get, in other words, Proportional Verse which can be close to Stress Verse, and verse which derives regularity simply from its timing of pauses, and the rise and fall, in patterns, of conversational pitch.

Free verse can, however, use the pause much more distinctively than this. Consider the space element in this passage.

> between green
> > mountains
> sings the flinger
> of
> fire beyond red rivers
>
> > e. e. cummings

Here, the pauses are of different duration. They can be measured by the eye, almost. The eye will drop down at the end of a line to a word that is placed to its right and below, and the pause will be felt as distinct and emphatic but not lengthy. If the eye is obliged to travel a long way to find the next word, however, or has difficulty in finding it, then the pause is magnified and the suspense element in the poem increased. Many *vers libre* poets over-use the suspense factor, and are liable to create what may convince us as poetry by what amounts to another version of the *special voice* plot of the writers of incantations. If we read the sentence, 'The mouse sat in the sandbox cleaning its whiskers' we may feel we are in the territory of Beatrix Potter. What happens, however, if we relineate it as:

> the
> mouse
> sat
> > in the
> > > sand-
> > > box
> cleaning
> its
> whisk-
> > > ers.

We could argue that this spacing has made us pay so much attention to each syllable that we must necessarily justify our effort by assuming it to have been lavished upon something important. We may also argue that splitting up the statement into small fragments has emphasized the smallness of the mouse, the delicacy of its movement, and, in a way, implied affection by being rather delicately whimsical.

Certainly there are tricks that can be played with

SPACE

and
the
stack-
ing
of
words
in
col-
umns

or,

(EvEn

GiVinG ThEm
purely
(arbitrary)

SIGN - I - FICA - NCE

by
typo (GRAPH) ical   de-
                        VICES.

The furtherest point of this has been reached in Concrete Poetry,
where the poem is, most often, simply a typographical design making
use of the words which either embody the meaning of that design or
reflect upon it. Here are one or two of these:

Original Sin at the Water Hole
asp
        on
                taneousobstreperousos
        tentatiousstentorianosmos
        isof hys
        tericallysnorting possesofs
        portingshehippopotamusses
        pottingalittlefloatin
                        g
                        asp!
                        Edwin Morgan

crickets
crickess
cricksss

```
cricssss
crisssss
crssssss
csssssss
ssssssss
sssssts
sssssets
sssskets
sssckets
ssickets
srickets
crickets
```

                            Aram Saroyan

```
wwww
wwww
· · · ·
waww
wakw
wake
· · · ·
walw
walk
```

                      Aram Saroyan

This, in my view, is great fun as a game, but has not got a lot to do with poetry. Nevertheless, one must be aware that such devices are available, for once in a while one may wish to use them constructively in order to indicate an implication, or a way of reading a poem that cannot be done in any other way. e. e. cummings made use of typographical games for both comic and serious purposes. Some of his poems are visual in the way that concrete poetry is. Some, however, use these devices to solve real literary problems, as in the following patch of dialect, which would not give us the tone of voice or rhythm and pitch he wished without its oddities of spelling and arrangement.

        Jimmie's got a goil
                        goil
                          goil,
                            Jimmie
        's got a goil and
        she coitnly can shimmie

> when you see her shake
> > > shake
> > > > shake,
> > > > > when
> you see her shake a
> shimmie how you wish that you was Jimmie.

Cummings retains in his poetry the speaking voice. The flow of speech matters to him. Other poets, however, have chosen to abandon the ordinary syntactical shapes. This means that the poems have to derive their rhythmic authority much more from the intellectual content of the words and from the visual manipulation of space than from our interpreting a persona or a given social situation, as we did with the opening of *Bishop Bloughram's Apology* by Browning. The ideogrammatic method is, really, the image list of our first chapter writ large. It is also, quite often, a matter of verbal collage. Consider these two passages from Pound's *Cantos* . . .

> 'We call *all* foreigners frenchies'
> and the egg broke in Cabranez' pocket,
> > thus making history. Basil says
> they beat drums for three days
> till all the drumheads were busted
> > (simple village fiesta)
> and as for his life in the Canaries . . .
> Possum observed that the local folk dance
> was danced by the same dancers in divers localities
> > in political welcome . . .
> the technique of demonstration
> > Cole studied that (not G. D. H., Horace)
> 'You will find' said old André Spire,
> that every man on that board (Crédit Agricole)
> has a brother-in-law . . .
> > > *Canto LXXXI*

> 'Called thrones, balascio or topaze'
> Erigena was not understood in his time
> 'which explains, perhaps, the delay in condemning him':
> And they went looking for Manicheans
> And found, so far as I can make out, no Manicheans
> So they dug for, and damned Scotus Erigena
> 'Authority comes from right reason
> > never the other way on'

Hence the delay in condemning him
Aquinas head down in a vacuum,
      Aristotle which way in a vacuum ?
      not quite in a vacuum.
Sacrum, sacrum, inluminatio coitu.
Lo Sordels si fo di Mantovana
      of a castle named Goito.
'Five castles!
'Five castles!'
      (king giv' him five castles)
'And what the hell do I know about dye-works ?!'
                         Canto XXXVI

These passages are, of course, very allusive and therefore difficult immediately to comprehend. Nevertheless, it is easy to see that the ideogrammatic method has resulted in giving us a dramatic impression of one man's mind ranging easily and confidently over a series of associated phenomena in an attempt to present a theme from all possible angles.

Are there any exercises which can help one to master any of these various techniques ? There are a number. One of the problems in handling free verse is to learn where most effectively to place the pauses. It is interesting to have a friend write out an unfamiliar free verse poem, and then to attempt to lineate it. The resultant version often differs from the poet's own, and the differences are instructive. Writing out newspaper passages in this manner can also be instructive. The best exercise, however, is to read a passage of writing aloud into a tape recorder, and then, on playing it back, mark the pauses that you yourself make in speaking the poem. Often you will discover that the natural breath pauses, the instinctive groupings you have made, break up the passage into units which are related to each other by having equivalent numbers of stresses or even of words. Such groupings sometimes run counter to the way in which you had thought to arrange the passage on the page. Consider the following poem by Leonard Cohen, presented as prose:

> I almost went to bed without remembering the
> four white violets I put in the button-hole of your
> green sweater and how I kissed you then and you
> kissed me shy as though I'd never been your lover

If I lineate this according to the way I wish to speak it, I get:

> I almost went to bed without remembering
> the four white violets

I put in the button-hole
of your green sweater
and how I kissed you then
and you kissed me
shy
as though I'd never been your lover.

Looking this over, I see that I do also pause after the word *bed*, and I emphasize, for dramatic effect, the words *your lover*, and make a longer than average pause before the first *and*.

I almost went to bed
without remembering
the four white violets
I put in the button-hole
of your green sweater

and how I kissed you then
and you kissed me
shy
as though I'd never been
your lover.

Cohen's own version runs:

I almost went to bed
without remembering
the four white violets
I put in the button-hole
of your green sweater

and how I kissed you then
and you kissed me
shy, as though I'd
never been your lover

The penultimate line of this version uses syntactical suspense, but also dramatic suspense; it is as if the speaker hesitates minutely before making his act of recollection. The putting of *shy* at the beginning of the line makes it easier to hear its assonance with *I'd* and downplays a word that might otherwise be too emphatic. The poem is not truly free, but stress verse. The stresses run: 3, 2, 3, 3, 2/ 2, 3, 2, 3, as long as one recognizes that the interpretation demands emphasis upon the *you* and the *me* in *you kissed me*, and that it is the word *almost* which carries the most stress in the first line, the *I* being hardly noticeable. This spacing according both to interpretation and natural breath pause is not too difficult to learn. Spacing for purely intellectual emphasis is more difficult.

The best way to learn to handle both metrical and free verse is to set oneself tasks that involve the solving of particular technical problems. One might, for example, decide to write a passage in which metrical and free verse are set off against one another, as thus:

> Where's the eye?
> The eye's in the sty.
> The ear's not here
> Beneath the hair.
> When I took off my clothes
> To find a nose,
> There was only one shoe
> For the waltz of To,
> The pinch of Where.

> Time for the flat-headed man. I recognize that listener,
> Him with the platitudes and rubber doughnuts,
> Melting at the knees, a varicose horror.
> Hello, hello. My nerves knew you, dear boy.
> Have you come to unhinge my shadow?

This passage from Theodore Roethke's poem *The Shape of the Fire*, is extremely irrational and dream-like. The shift in manner has added to its emotional disturbance. One might, however, choose to tackle this exercise in a more straightforward manner, and make the poem of a dialogue between a metrical and an ametrical voice, thus using the dialogue poetic plot I suggested earlier.

There are, however, no short cuts to technical expertise. One can only study the masterworks of other writers and attempt to understand how to imitate their excellence, without copying their mannerisms or parrotting their attitudes. One might study T. S. Eliot's dramatic monologues to discover how to mingle conversational free verse with stricter and more rhetorical forms. One might examine the structures of Wallace Stevens in *The Man with the Blue Guitar*, and in the *Notes Towards a Supreme Fiction* to observe how he handles a highly intellectual diction in lines that are fluid yet metrical, rhetorical yet easily spoken. Study is, indeed, the only way to tackle the problem, but the study should involve imitation as well as analysis, and consideration of meaning should take a second place to consideration of structure.

SIX Approaches to Form

It is my belief that no poet can achieve real success unless he learns to understand the nature of existing forms and genres.

Let us first of all consider *Abstract Forms.* These are structural formulae which have been exploited so frequently that one can quite reasonably provide rules for using them. I am thinking of the *sonnet,* the *villanelle,* the *sestina,* the *canzone,* the *rondeau,* the *triolet,* the *pantoum,* and the *ballade.* All these forms have definite lengths and in this they differ from what I would like to call, not abstract forms, but genre forms, in which, while there are structural formulae to be followed, there are no rigid limitations as to length. Such genre forms are the *ballad,* the *ode,* and the *eclogue.* Of these three, the ode is the most difficult to define, for there have been many poems called odes which appear to owe little or nothing to the form as used by Pindar and Horace whose work led to the establishment of the ode as an important mode of writing, at least in the minds of English poets. While abstract forms do not, in general, demand any limitation of subject matter or tone, except in as much as these may derive from the formal limitations involved, genre forms do involve limitations of subject matter. After all, a poem written in ballad-metre need not be a ballad at all, and an ode is not an ode unless it involves elements of apostrophe, and high seriousness.

When we move to consider genre itself we are in even more difficulties. I would suggest that the word *genre* may be taken as simply describing the way in which poems can be grouped together in terms of their attitudes and social functions. Thus we can call satire a genre, even while we can make no statement as to the form in which satire should be presented. One may have a satiric ballad, or a satiric sonnet, quite easily. The satiric ballad, however, will also be affected by the limitations of subject matter of the ballad as well as limited by the attitude of satire. Epic is another genre. Again, it is rather the attitude than the subject matter or form that is limited, though it is generally presumed that epics should be written in high serious diction, be of considerable

4+

length, and involve a narrative plot in which the destiny of a nation, or community, is involved, and emotions of nobility, terror, and pity are evoked. Elegy is another genre, but here again, there is only one simple limitation; an elegy is a poem which comments upon, or derives from consideration of, the death of somebody. It may be satirical, or lyrical, and there is no reason why we should not have elegiac villanelles or sonnets or even ballades. The genre 'lyric' is hard to define, for while it once referred to poems actually intended to be sung, it has now come to refer merely to short poems. Nevertheless, we may perhaps define a lyric as a short poem which suggests song, and leave it at that.

Not all poems fit into these long-established genre and form categories, of course, and the twentieth century has provided a new series of categories in order to clarify the picture. Some of these identify historical movements which have given rise to particular poetic attitudes and practices. Imagist poetry and surrealist poetry are easy to recognize and label, even though imagism as a movement may be over, and surrealism has given way to what has been termed neo-surrealism. Symbolism and objectivisim are two other genre categories that derive from past movements but are not commonly regarded as merely historical terms like Augustanism, or so completely vague in their application as to be comparatively useless, like Romanticism. There are also other terms which do not really describe either genres or genre forms, and yet refer to easily identifiable modes and attitudes. These are the dramatic monologue, the pastoral, the hymn, and the allegory.

The value of knowing these terms and understanding them is considerable. It enables the practising poet to gain a clear perspective upon the past and the present, and to see how certain problems have been solved at different periods and by different poets. In surveying the sonnet, for example, he can see how Shakespeare made use of the form to balance statement with counter-statement in an argumentative manner. He can observe that the Petrarchan sonnet, as handled by others, provides more fluidity than the Shakespearean form in the sestet, and ends less aggressively and epigrammatically. He can note, too, how in the nineteenth century, poets began to write near-sonnets, in which they made use of the basic formula of the sonnet but altered the established rhyme-scheme, as did Shelley in *Ozymandias*. He can note how some poets lengthened the form to sixteen lines, while, again, keeping its basic pattern, and study the handling of this *extended sonnet* by Meredith. He may then turn to the twentieth century, and in Merril Moore's sonnets and near-sonnets, and those of John Berryman see how material and diction which earlier poets would have thought unsuitable are exploited so that, sometimes, there is a tension set up between the expected and conventional attributes of the form and the new approach.

The apprentice poet would be well advised to study poetic forms and genres in the way I have outlined, but only if that study leads him towards imaginative excitement as well as intellectual comprehension. This book, however, is about the practice, as distinct from the history, of poetry and it is not its function to do more than point in this particular direction. Nevertheless, there are some points which need to be made before we can go any farther.

Abstract forms in poetry are by no means all of the same kind. One kind, in particular, separates itself off from all the others by dealing inevitably in one particular mode of vision. I am thinking here of the forms, villanelle, sestina, and canzone, which, because they are constructed in terms of the repetition of lines and words in established patterns, inevitably produce effects of obsession. As many poems originate in obsession these forms deserve attention rather more than such slighter forms as the triolet, rondeau, roundel, and rondel, which rarely amount to more than *jeux d'esprit*, or such forms as the sonnet and ballade which seem now to be crippled under the weight of past achievements.

If one examines the way in which obsessive forms have been handled and varied, even in the summary manner in which I have done so in another part of this book for the sake of those who are excited by such things, one is liable to come up with the notion that it might be possible to invent new ones simply by playing with the notion of verbal repetition. In a quatrain, for example, one can use the same word for the first and third line. In some cases this approximates to *rime riche*. The poem derives from this a slow deliberation and a certain ease. Here is my own *Swans Sleeping*.

All the swans are asleep, and I remember
Gogarty giving the Liffey a pair of swans,
remember the children of Lir, remember
Leda under those white beating wings,

as a man remembers what there is
of childhood left in stray corners of the house
his age has made habitual. It is,
perhaps, a condition of the evening's peace,

here by the sauntering couples, that no thought
or myth or dream should risk a turning back
to those absurd heroics, yet I had thought
so many here had known the city's wrack,

Pearse's set face, all those broken necks,
the looting rabblement, the spraying guns,
no swans could ever sleep, but would curve necks
continually through greens and browns and duns

of moving water, feeding on the flow
as Jove stooped into Leda, to provide
love, war, and prophecy, a continual flow
of high homeric gestures to deride

the easy smiling couples that stroll past
the root-gripped river bank with idle stares,
as we, too, stroll, engrossed in a dead past
between the violent shadows of the trees.

A more complicated exercise is to attempt to write a reversible poem, in which the last stanza is the first one reversed. This can be made even more complicated by insisting that some, or all, of the words beginning the lines are also repeated.

Such exercises as these are, perhaps, only word games, but they breed facility and are excellent discipline. The most useful outcome of them, however, is the discovery of basic principles and ways of handling refrains and verbal repetition.

It is, perhaps, only when one has mastered rhyme, rhythm, diction, and some abstract forms that one can begin to discover one's own individual vision, for that vision, if one is a poet, is inseparable from the poetry itself. It does not exist apart from the poems in which it is discovered, even though it may owe a great deal to one's studies of philosophy or religion, or to one's own experiences. Discovering one's own vision is often, however, a matter of asking the right questions, and some of these questions can only be adequately formulated if one has surveyed poetry and poetic forms with some thoroughness.

What kind of questions must one ask oneself? The most important one usually begins with the words *What if*. Let us take the case of the young poet obscurely troubled by a feeling of despair, as all young poets are from time to time troubled. He feels that the world is dark and he is alone. Everything that happens seems to contribute to this feeling. If the poet has grown familiar with obsessive forms he may, in recognizing his own obsession, say 'What if I use my simple feeling of despair as a repeated line that applies to everything that happens around me?' He may then write:

> The world is dark. I am alone.
> > The houses tremble in the light
> > that fails before the nearing night.
> The world is dark. I am alone.

What if he then attempts a variation, a very small one?

> I am alone. The world is dark.
> > The children run and play and shout,
> > but death will blot their pastimes out.
> The world is dark. I am alone.

What if he now alters it a little, realizing that the world cannot be dark if the houses tremble in the light and the children are still playing. It is *his* world which is dark. Moreover, it is in *his* world that he is alone. What if he changes the word *world*?

> The room is dark. I am alone.
> The houses tremble in the light
> that fails before the nearing night.
> The room is dark. I am alone.

> I am alone. The room is dark.
> The children run and play and shout,
> but death will blot their pastimes out.
> The room is dark. I am alone.

The question *What if* has led him to present an obsession in an obsessive form that, in point of fact, owes something to the refrain techniques of established abstract forms.

He may, continuing with this poem, or simply exploring possible variations, decide to use another line as refrain at this point.

> The children run and play and shout.
> > I watch them from my upper room
> > explicit in the gathering gloom.
> The children run and play and shout.

What if we alter the rhythm by having a comma at the end of this stanza?

> The children run and play and shout,
>
> unheeding all those shadows thrown
> around them in the failing light,
> that gathers everything to night.
> The room is dark. I am alone.

This needs considerable revision to turn it into a poem, but it has succeeded in doing two things. First, it has responded to a formal challenge by producing a definite vision; secondly it has created a form which may, after some work, have all the advantages of the villanelle without risking those comparisons which the label villanelle would certainly cause to be made.

Another poet might ask a slightly different kind of question. He might say, 'What if I steal the idea of the rondeau and use that repeated opening phrase?'

> Why should I, now the thing is done
> pay false regrets to anyone
> beneath the red-faced sweating sun?
> Why should I?
>
> Why trouble, now the man is dead,
> with pouring tributes on his head.
> What good are flowers dropped on lead?
> Why trouble?
>
> Why wonder about where he's gone.
> Some say the spirit travels on,
> I only know the thing is done.
> Why wonder?

In this kind of exercise the pressure of the form can result in a statement or vision which surprises the writer by showing him something he did not previously know to be one of his attitudes. The form directs the vision. It may lead to the discovery of the new subject matter, or it may lead to the originating of a form that can be used for future work.

Much of this work does not, of course, result in poems that matter a great deal. It does often, however, lead to notebook material that can be used later. Suppose, for example, that, surveying the sestina and canzone, one says, 'What if all the end words were the same?'

> I bring you this in pity and in love.
> I make it yours because the face I love
> is sad tonight and pity comes with love
> But what is Love ?

This formula might well be used for other stanzas and better ones.

If form directs vision, it is of course equally true that vision directs form. Edgar Allen Poe's essay on *The Rationale of Verse* in which he purports to explain how he wrote *The Raven* illustrates this interdependence to some extent, though Poe is inclined to emphasize formal problems rather than imaginative ones. One cannot easily, however, discuss the way in which a particular and compulsive vision creates form, for if that vision is intense it almost certainly will block out awareness of much else that is going on, and the formal problems are likely to be solved intuitively, or by a process of trial and error that has very little conscious about it.

The struggle towards form can best be seen in a poet's worksheets. Thomas Kinsella's poem *Mirror in February* is regarded as one of his most successful. The worksheets for it reveal clearly the struggle of the poet to find form and expression for a vision which is clearly present from the very first draft.

THOMAS KINSELLA: WORKSHEETS

I

MIRROR IN FEBRUARY

washing, glasses removed, I see myself
                                        more
suddenly,   harder , solider, /un-

innocent than I have yet believed

This orchard (country house)

"to wh., for the time being, I keep

    returning."

Trees cropped, freshened, to enter

    a new phase of bearing.

Lime on the clay, trailed by

    the "horny hand".

ageing, my span will be

    included.

end : not young, but a man
                                        find myself
A C.S. at the age of Christ

II

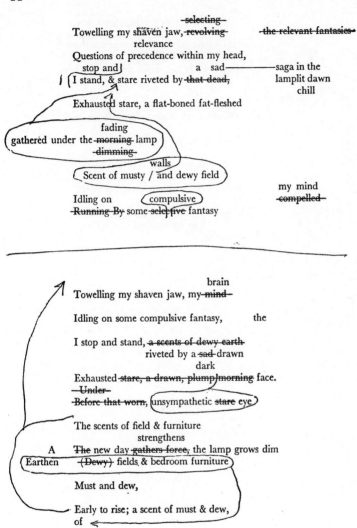

Towelling my shaven jaw, ~~revolving~~   ~~the relevant fantasies~~
                              ~~selecting~~
                              relevance
Questions of precedence within my head,
        stop and}   a sad————saga in the
| [I stand, & stare riveted by ~~that dead,~~   lamplit dawn
                                                      chill

Exhausted stare, a flat-boned fat-fleshed

                fading
gathered under the ~~morning~~ lamp
              ~~dimming~~
                              walls
    Scent of musty / and dewy field

Idling on   (compulsive)   my mind
~~Running By~~ some ~~selective~~ fantasy   ~~compelled~~

---

                              brain
Towelling my shaven jaw, my ~~mind~~

Idling on some compulsive fantasy,   the

I stop and stand, ~~a scents of dewy earth~~
                  riveted by a ~~sad~~ drawn
                              dark
Exhausted ~~stare, a drawn, plump} morning~~ face.
~~Under~~
~~Before that worn,~~ (unsympathetic ~~stare~~ eye)

The scents of field & furniture
                  strengthens
    A   ~~The~~ new day ~~gathers force,~~ the lamp grows dim
Earthen   ~~(Dewy)~~ fields & bedroom furniture)

Must and dew,

Early to rise; a scent of must & dew,
of

III

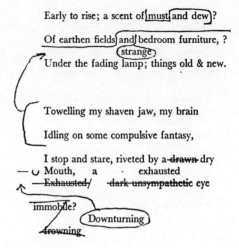

Early to rise; a scent of must and dew ?

Of earthen fields and bedroom furniture, ?
                    strange
Under the fading lamp; things old & new.

Towelling my shaven jaw, my brain

Idling on some compulsive fantasy,

I stop and stare, riveted by a drawn dry
— ∪ Mouth,   a   ·   exhausted
    Exhausted/   dark unsympathetic eye

immobile?
              Downturning
frowning

I V

unsympathetic

the inscrutable familiar

Aided in their external ~~view perhaps~~
way to see
~~of~~ — The mirror of a soul that has endured

I marvel at the changed familiar

atrophy
As much of simple wearing down as Christ —
being
times attrition
time & consciousness

~~By the renewing nudge of strangeness~~

Again, it seems, my eys have
been made clear
Were in this ~~prsperous~~
of ~~this country milieu~~, the ~~soil~~ my system cries for, fruitful place,

To wh., for the time being, I keep returning
my steps return
(this — ∪ house)

disentangled
Now apple / And pears are striped
the trees / for better bearing
Fruit trees, after years' neglect, ~~are stripped,~~

Cropped, for better bearing (renewed with)
Chopped boughs

Lime trailed on the black soil from a horny hand

indestructible clay
The all but immortal soil)
the cloth
I fold my towel:
... Let The flesh ~~flinches~~ But The path is clear;
point
next redoubt
~~Unrenewable,~~ simple truth

Not young and not renewable, but ~~a~~ man.

I fold my towel with what grace I can

V

is
     that   undergone
I marvel at a ~~further~~ change ~~accomplished~~

A dour portrait unsympathetic

Distanced by the   taste
     my   I have faced   ~~at least~~
The mirror of ~~a~~ soul that ~~has endured~~ (observed)

As much of simple atrophy as Christ.

Again, it seems my eyes have been md. clear(ed)
    crumbling a   of growth
Here in this ~~fruitful~~ place, this (— ∪ house)

To which, for the time being, I keep returning.
    ~~with the cruel action of~~
So   with a touch of strangeness
~~Caught;~~ ~~in surroundings not my own~~
    ~~shorn of the familiar~~

        stacks
Now, after years' neglect, the ~~apple~~ trees are stripped
                    boughs
  pears   second   ~~(piles)~~ heaps of brittle ~~limbs~~
~~And trees are stripped~~ for better bearing; ~~limbs~~
    from about their hidden youth   ~~the~~
~~Lopped & disentangled,~~ ~~Wood renews;~~ ~~lie stacked for/ burning~~
          ~~are~~
Lime leavens the indestructible ~~clay,~~ all but immortal soil
  quick   this
~~The/~~ flesh ~~shudders~~ in such ~~company,~~

How shd. the flesh not shudder? Yet, warm-
          evanescent
I fold my towel with what grace I can,

Not young, & not renewable, but man.
      death
    ~~a block~~ to the
~~Stiffening~~   green blood
   ~~Arranged the limbs~~ ~~within~~
~~That choked their hidden youth~~ lie neatly chopped

VI

chopped down to free the green blood

Now, after year's neglect, the trees are ~~stripped~~ cut

Back
~~To the quick~~

For better bearing. Stacks of ~~brittle~~ boughs

~~too brittle for that green~~ ~~stand~~ lie about
~~Death to the green blood~~ ~~lie neatly chopped~~
~~leavens~~ The
And lime slakes On black, immortal ~~soil~~
clay.

The empty
~~Leavening the~~
~~Lime on~~ rows

Wait for the sun

In this slow, indestructible company

How shd. the flesh not shudder? Yet

I fold my towel with what (grace?) I can,

Not young & not renewable, but man.

No longer young

VII

MIRROR IN FEBRUARY

        rising   rain
Early to rise; a scent of must and ~~dew~~

Of bedroom furniture and earthen fields   sluggish
                            ← Fills the ~~sleepy~~ morning
(I towel) (~~Towelling~~ my ~~smooth~~-shaven jaw)— my brain

Idling on some compulsive fantasy —
  Half dressed)
  Under the fading lamp)   ~~I stand~~   ~~and,~~ / ~~then~~ I stand
  → stand) ; ~~then desist suddenly.~~ ~~halt my hand and stop,~~ and sta
I stop and stare, riveted by ~~a dry~~
  ~~That~~   that
  ~~A~~ dry Downturning mouth; (a dark exhausted eye) I turn to the window?
                   sharply   .... ~~passed by.~~)
         (and heave a   sigh)
So, by a lingering touch of strangeness, kept   of 3rd. verse
            attention to the passing world)
Fresh   ~~my eyes~~ refreshed   heavy
            . ~~are~~   fleshed
          heart is forced to learn
Again, it seems, my ~~eyes have been made clear~~
        ~~oddly,~~ quietly
Here in this [house, a] crumbling place of growth,
                  return
Aware)
~~I see that I have~~ To which for the time being I ~~keep returning.~~   s
~~looked my on~~   Deep in (~~shows I have~~)   have
~~seen the last of~~ And know the mirror of my soul has faced (~~on it~~ is traced)
  ~~youth~~

As much of simple atrophy as Christ.
And I have drifted to the age of

                    cut
Now after years' neglect the trees are ~~stripped~~
  Back
  / For better bearing. Stacks of boughs,   renewing sprir
                               Renewing seaso
Chopped down to free the green wood, lie about.
         Opens black)
The black Immortal soil./ ~~The~~ empty rows
                      — replenishing
Wait for the sun. In this revivifying company
        my
How should the flesh not shudder ? Yet...

I fold my towel with what grace I can,

Not young and not renewable, but man.

                         simple
(~~And So~~
~~Aware that~~ I have looked my last on /youth)

VIII

MIRROR IN FEBRUARY

The day begins, ~~amid~~ ~~among shells~~ *with scent*

Early to rise; ~~a scent~~ of must and rain,

Of bedroom furniture and ~~earthen~~ fields.   *gaping* *country air.*   *dewy*

Under the fading lamp, half dressed, — my brain

Idling on some compulsive fantasy —

I towel my shaven jaw, *I stand,* and stare,   ields   *and stop,*

Riveted by a dark exhausted eye,

A dry downturning mouth.   aware.

? So ~~I~~ *we* have looked ~~my~~ *our* very last on youth.

? Again, *it seems,* ~~my heart is forced~~ to learn.   *that it is time*

Here in this quietly crumbling place of growth

To which, for the time being, I return.

I approach the window

mirror of soul   faced

As much   Christ

IX

Again it seems that it is time to learn,

Here in this quietly crumbling place of growth

To which, for the time being, I return.

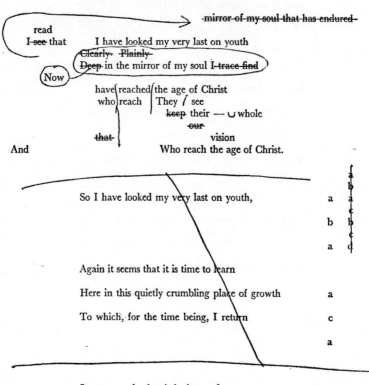

~~mirror of my soul that has endured~~

read
I ~~see~~ that I have looked my very last on youth
~~Clearly. Plainly~~
~~Deep~~ in the mirror of my soul I ~~trace~~ find

Now

have reached the age of Christ
who reach They see
~~keep~~ their — ◡ whole
~~our~~
~~that~~ vision
And Who reach the age of Christ.

So I have looked my very last on youth,   a

Again it seems that it is time to learn   a

Here in this quietly crumbling place of growth   a

To which, for the time being, I return   c

a

•It seems again that it is time to learn,

Here in this quietly crumbling place of growth

To which, for the time being, I return.

Now plainly in the mirror of my soul

I read that I have looked my last on youth,

And little more. And are they not made whole

Who reach the age of Christ?

X

How shd. the flesh not quail that, span for span,
Must ~~bare the fearfully quick~~ to be embraced?
(stand as) wearily

3rd. stanza

Trees cut back to the quick

Ground ~~graved and~~ broken
       o

Faced with such br~~u~~tal cruel necessities for / growth
(Spring &)

How shd. the flesh not shudder? → to stop my mind
                                   back to the quick
       (Yes, but my response also is)

Fold my towel . . .

       (Terror, pity)
                Blank

~~Outside,~~ — in a soil   neglected
~~the soil below,~~ torn loose for seed, ~~the~~/trees
Cut back for better bearing, stain defaced .
                loose
                torn up for better bearing, trees

~~The gutted~~ In Soil that it may bear,

ground   ~~The limed & broken grounds,~~ the trees, (groping)
crushed &
wounded to   Are ~~stripped & broken~~ to the quick

                lime burns white   ~~stripped~~
        Below, ~~the land is limed,~~ the trees ~~are cut~~   a
        Cut free of years' neglect
Cruelly Back for ~~better bearing~~   defaced   b

        In this ⌣ of ~~cruel~~ necessities   a
                frail   though span
        How shd. the/flesh not shudder? — ⌣ an   c   wiser.
                cuts   (than)
        Yes, but the mind/strips/also to the quick (waste) ast b
                                ?
        I fold my towel with what grace I can,   c

Not —⌣— but man.   c

        suffering (—its—)
        — Lie entangled in their —
        Spring is a . brute)
        ~~The world is full of harsh~~ (necessities

        Spring   laced taste haste
              (Helpless)   waste   placed
                                        graced chaste
        ~~An honest mind that cuts till it has ceased~~.

~~Stiffly~~ Naked) ~~Shapeless~~   emplaced

        Outside, (after years' neglect, the ~~apple~~ trees
                        and
        ~~cut back~~ for better bearing & ~~stand~~ defaced,
            are hacked)

X I   MIRROR IN FEBRUARY

The day dawns, with scent of must and rain,
Of opened soil, dark trees, dry bedroom air.
Under the fading lamp, half dressed — my brain
Idling on some compulsive fantasy —
I towel my shaven jaw and stop, and stare,
Riveted by a dark exhausted eye,
A dry downturning mouth.

It seems again that it is time to learn,
    ~~⌣ and~~   untiring,
~~Here~~ In this ~~quietly~~ crumbling place of growth
To which, for the time being, I return.

(Now?)   Plainly in the mirror of my soul
I read that I have looked my last on youth,
And little more; and they are not grown whole
That reach the age of Christ.

          the wakening trees
          appear the trees,

         mutilated   (their shapes)
~~Slowly outside~~ ~~Below~~ my window,
~~below my~~ Now   ⌣ —   ~~bare ageing~~
  ~~Hapless after~~ (years' neglect,) the trees
            ~~awake all neatly spaced~~
~~Their arms~~ Hacked for ~~better bearing~~ — ~~stand~~ defaced, ~~renewed~~
      clean   (emerge)   youth has   ~~made young~~
Appear, Suffering their brute necessities;   Yet youth sufficed
                       it has
And How should the flesh not quail, that, span for span,
     Is mutilated more?   though, span for span
  ~~Must wait as many dawns to be embraced?~~ dumb
                      ~~in slow~~ distaste
I fold my towel with what grace I can,

Not young, and not renewable, but man.

                       My wound untraced,

    fruits
It flowers a hundredfold from every (sliced)?

Its fruit from every cut cd. not be priced   TK

Wounds that fructify   sufficed
As fructifying wounds
        disfigurements

A hundredth of those wounds wd. have sufficed
         have not sufficed

XII

*Mirror in February**

The day dawns with scent of must and rain,
Of opened soil, dark trees, dry bedroom air.
Under the fading lamp, half dressed — my brain
Idling on some compulsive fantasy —
I towel my shaven jaw and stop, and stare,
Riveted by a dark exhausted eye,
A dry downturning mouth.

It seems again that it is time to learn,
In this untiring, crumbling place of growth
To which, for the time being, I return.
Now plainly in the mirror of my soul
I read that I have looked my last on youth
And little more; for they are not made whole
That reach the age of Christ.

Below my window the awakening trees,
Hacked clean for better bearing, stand defaced
Suffering their brute necessities,
And how should the flesh not quail that span for span
Is mutilated more? In slow distaste
I fold my towel with what grace I can,
Not young and not renewable, but man.

*From Thomas Kinsella, *Downstream*, Dolmen Press, 1962.

The preceding worksheets are reproduced from the
pages of *The Malahat Review*.

It is obvious from these worksheets that Kinsella was working at first without any clear notion of form, but that by the time he reached worksheet 9 he was thinking in terms of rhyme-schemes, if not before. The awareness of form, in fact, only slowly clarified into certainty.

Kinsella's worksheets may help us to see how much sheer hard work is involved in the making of a poem that, beginning with a vision, then goes on to give that vision disciplined form.

Not all poems, however, begin with even the faintest notion of their subject matter. Sometimes one may begin with a tune. Paul Valéry wrote:

> My own poem *Le Cimitière Marin* came to me in the form of a certain rhythm which is that of the ten-syllable French line arranged in the proportion of 4 to 6. I had not, at first, the slightest idea of what content was to fill that form. Gradually, a number of floating words began to solidify. Little by little they determined my subject, and the labour (a very long labour) of composition was forced upon me. Another poem, *La Pythie*, began with an eight-syllable line the sound of which came of itself.

In this case the poet has found himself aware of the vehicle before being aware of its cargo. He has intuited the possibilities of a form and then continued to explore it. When W. S. Graham commenced work on his long poem *The Dark Dialogues* he began by deciding to write in a three-beat line. In this form he wrote hundreds of lines, using the form as a journal. He wanted to find for himself a form in which he could say anything, and which therefore would permit subject matter to occur and develop as the writing continued. It was to be a form in which he could think and *think anything in*. I began my own long poem, *The Dark Window*, in a similar way. I chose a four-beat line, and every evening wrote a minimum of four lines about anything that came into my head. After ten days or so the different paragraphs began to point in a certain direction, and I found myself involved in a poem which took over six months to draft, and a further twelve months to complete.

It is, I think, fair to say that most poets begin their compositions with a notion of form, whether or not this is accompanied by images or, indeed, appears to arise from images. The notion may be very vague. William Empson wrote a large part of one of his villanelles before realizing that it was a villanelle that he was writing; he had, however, a sense of a form developing from the very beginning.

This apprehension of form is often composed of two parts. On the one hand the poet feels that whatever is occurring is speaking in a certain kind of voice. The voice may be one he feels to be characteristic of a shadowy persona, or it may be one that surprises him by its authority and mysteriousness. He listens to this voice and tries to write down a statement which, in vocabulary and in cadence, exactly embodies the voice he hears. Thus he finds himself with a diction and a rhythm. The persona which emerges from this first discovery then will make other formal characteristics necessary. The rhetorical authoritative voice that is speaking in a highly symbolic vocabulary is likely to make tightly knit rhyming verse essential. The sensitive, hesitant voice which begins with nuances rather than assertions and changes the speed and tone of its sentences as new notions occur, is likely to make a form of free verse, or loose blank verse inevitable. I remember myself once, when asking myself the question, 'How can I write a poem about Christmas?', hearing a voice in my head answer me with the words *Call me Ancient!* I could have taken this as advice to be followed and begun my poem with *Christmas is ancient* or something similar. The voice I heard, however, sounded itself so authoritative that instead I simply wrote down its own words and the poem developed as if I were taking dictation. I called the poem *Voice on a Birthday*.

> Call me ancient.
> I have years for teeth
> and gnaw the mountains.
> Every road's my spoor
> and every town my droppings.
> Keep me tracked.
> I go to earth before a
> stable door.
>
> I have no strategy
> but shame. This earth
> cannot protect me
> or disguise my smell,
> even distracts me
> with those kills whose bones
> are trampled in the mud
> about the stall.
>
> Yet here for seconds
> once I knelt, close-curled,
> unraked by hungers,
> and here wish to die
> if man can dig me out
> or find a way
> to dowse the cruel
> planet in the sky.

In writing this poem I was aware that the word *stable* was given ambiguity by its placing, because the pause before it gave one the sense that it carried a dramatic load of meaning. I was aware by the end of the second line that the vocabulary had to be tough, even a little brutal. I did not solve the poem's problems intellectually but intuitively. I *heard* the poem: I did not write it.

It may be useful to compare this poem with another which arrived in the same fashion, used the same first person technique, and was equally concerned with universals. Here, however, though the voice was authoritative, I *heard* it as thin in tone, almost reedy, and yet harsh. It was an inhuman voice and lacked the sensuality of the voice of the other poem. Moreover, it was insistent, needling, even mocking, and certainly not caught up in passion. It was intellectual, even sardonically objective and dispassionate.

> I am a monster.
> Among small
> crouching years
> I take up
>
> Death in my hand
> and Death shakes
> wild as a shrew.
> I pile bones
>
> high by the wall.
> I eat graves.
> Chanting,
> they bring me
> graves to eat.

I understood the poem to be spoken by *History* and so that is what I called the poem, and I dedicated it in memory of John F. Kennedy because it was my thinking about his assassination that brought the poem on.

If we look at these two poems we can see that the first is rhymed and that in each succeeding pair of two lines there are approximately five stresses. The general metrical character is iambic. It is therefore (if we read two lines as one) based upon iambic pentameter rhyming abcb, though this shape is disguised and distorted by frequent substitution and by its lineation. If we look at *History* we can see that it is unrhymed, and that most of the lines have two stresses each. The exception is the antepenultimate line *Chanting*, and perhaps the penultimate line also. The poem is unrhymed. The second and third stanzas are more regular than the first, as (if we read *Chanting, they bring me* as one line) we have four-word and three-word lines alternating 4/3, 4/3 in each stanza. The first stanza is rhythmically very similar to the second and third, however, even though it is not quite so regularly shaped.

The point here is that the *voice* of the poem created forms which are far from undisciplined, but which were not consciously concocted. The forms were, to use Coleridge's term, organic.

Nevertheless, it must be emphasized that a degree of formal awareness was present from the beginning in that knowledge of the characteristics of a poem's voice is also knowledge of some aspects of form.

The young poet is not likely at first to be able to listen to his voice with that watchful submissiveness necessary to giving it appropriate form. He is likely, indeed, to either impose the wrong form, or to be too slapdash. In either case the poem will be flawed, and may even come to a halt. Perhaps the only way to learn this listening is to artificially create a situation in which it can be practised. The student should be given a line of verse, or a statement, and asked to continue it in an appropriate manner. For example, one might begin with the statement, *'Hell,' said the Sergeant* taken from some thriller or other. What sort of thing could be said next ? The voice is, obviously, harsh. The diction (what there is of it) is simple. The rhythm, so far at least, is emphatic. One result of this exercise could be :

> 'Hell' said the Sergeant,
> This place stinks.
> The wall is black
> with wet and rot . . .

The student has here kept up the two-stress rhythm that the opening line implies, and has also stuck to forceful monosyllables. Suppose, however, that the first statement is :

> I did not know that he was dead

Here the tone is less harsh. The use of *did not* instead of *didn't* suggests that the voice is not inclined to speak over colloquially. It is, however, a rhythmical statement, and could be scanned as iambic tetrameter if one wished to do so.

One solution might read :

> I did not know that he was dead,
> that hero of my distant past;
> the newsprint shuddered as I read
> the history of despair and waste . . .

Another, however, might read :

> I did not know that he was dead,
> and when I heard the news recalled
> only the poised and golden head
>
> that mocked the follies of the world,
> as if the world were not for him.
> Now all that youthful warmth is cold . . .

In both cases the voice has led to formal verse ; in the first case iambic tetrameter rhyming abab, and in the second *terza rima*.

There is, finally, no route to poetry save through deliberate practice of the craft, and while such practice may prove tedious and laborious, it leads at last to an easy control of language and form which gives one the freedom to follow the compulsions of one's imagination without being hindered and obstructed by technical clumsiness.

SEVEN Staying in Business

Although discipline in the craft of verse may be essential for complete mastery of poetic techniques, such discipline is often debilitating to the imagination. One can easily become so conscious of technique that for a time, and perhaps for ever, one can be prevented from exploring original perceptions. It is therefore very important, while working on established forms, metres, and stanzas, also to develop other poetic muscles. It has been suggested that one way of avoiding frustration of the imagination is to use only frivolous themes for one's practice in strict verse. Unfortunately, if you do this, you grow to associate frivolity so strongly with these forms that it becomes impossible to work with them seriously. A better method is to alternate the practice of craft with the practice of free association exercises and the writing of a poetry journal.

A poetry journal is not quite like other journals. It does not (or should not) record complete thoughts. Indeed, it should consist of unfinished speculations, fragmentary notes of things seen, heard, and experienced, and as many obsessive notions and unanswered questions as possible, for a speculation carried to its conclusion in the prose of a journal may well be a speculation that has no need of poetic exploration.

The difference between an ordinary and a poetic journal can easily be shown. An ordinary journal entry might read:

Went to the Dodgers game with Joe and Sally. A good tussle. 16–8 to the Giants. Sally says they're getting married in June. She wants four kids. Afterwards went back to Joe's place and watched TV.

A poetic journal covering the same event might read:

Dodgers v. Giants. Big bodies swollen up. Like bears. or gladiators, Man imitating animals? Watching the tribal battle, a girl about to get married. What if she thinks of children like this, heroic children? Something elemental here. Blood lust? Or the myth of the Giant and, maybe, dodging little Jack. Nursery tale, is it? What if we start with the girl—make her slight, slim, even frail, watching the big bodies. Where will it go? Think of bear images. Of nursery tales. Teddy bears contracted with grizzlies;

113

The poetic journal speculates in terms of the possible imaginative uses of phenomena. It ignores factual detail in order to concentrate upon mythic or metaphoric possibilities. Sometimes it simply records images.

Gerard Manley Hopkins wrote in his journal for 1869:

> A few days before Sept. 25 a fine sunrise seen from no. 1, the upstairs bedroom—: long skeins of meshy grey cloud a little ruddled underneath, not quite level but aslant, rising from left to right, and down on the left one more solid balk or bolt than the rest with a high-blown crest of flix or fleece above it.

This type of entry gives one not only images to use, but also a new vocabulary. In the journal one can present alternative words without discomfort, and one can risk extremities of expression that might frighten one in other pieces of writing. Hopkins also used his journal for straight vocabulary notes. Again the entry is from 1869:

> Br. Wells calls a grindstone a *grindlestone*. To *lead* north-country for to *carry* (a field of hay, etc.) *Geet* north-country preterite of *get*: 'he geet agate agoing'. Tress sold 'top and lop' Br. Rickaby told me and suggests *top* is the higher, outer, and lighter wood good for firing only, *lop* the stem and bigger boughs when the rest has been lopped off used for timber.

> Br. Wells calls the white bryony Dead Creeper, because it kills what it entwines.

Many poets also use their journal and notebooks for technical matters, for theories of poetry, and for other allied subjects. Even more, however, use them for philosophical statements, for self-analysis, and for questions which sometimes appear trivial and yet which are pregnant with possibilities for the poet. Thus in his notebooks Baudelaire wrote:

> Eternelle supériorité du dandy.
> Qu'est-ce que le Dandy?

It is important, in keeping a journal of this kind, not to keep it too regularly. Otherwise it may itself become an important creation and more important than poems. Different people have different necessities. In my view, however, it is valuable to keep such a journal when travelling, or after new experiences, or, when one begins to feel arid and uncreative, for a week or two at a time. Quite frequently a journal entry will lead one into writing a poem, and the journal itself will be discontinued as a consequence.

The poetic journal is only one type of notebook, of course, and there is another, equally valuable. This is the personal anthology. In it one should write out the poems one finds especially important, or technically interesting, or, in some way, sympathetic to one's own vision. A very considerable number of poets have made anthologies of one kind or another, and have published them. Perhaps the most interesting are those which deal with no particular historical period but take the whole field of poetry for their territory. Some of these include prose as well as poetry. These often include items that cannot easily be found elsewhere. Of such collections the best to date are, perhaps, Robert Bridges' *The Spirit of Man* and Walter de la Mare's *Love*, and *Behold, the Dreamer*; Victor Gollancz's *Testament of Grace*, though not compiled by a poet, and directed very much towards the presentation of spiritual rather than aesthetic vision, is also enormously stimulating.

Many poets, however, anthologize along more conventional lines. Of living poets, a large number have made anthologies, either of the work of their contemporaries, or of the work of some period of the past. Among these are Robert Graves, W. H. Auden, Anne Ridler, Oscar Williams, Donald Hall, James Reeves, Charles Causley. The making of anthologies, especially personal anthologies in which literary history does not matter, is also the exploring of one's own sensibility, and the studying of those poems felt to be in some way, masterworks.

Some poets choose to devote their attention to a particular aspect of this necessary activity. Many make selections of poets whom they most admire, or poets whom they wish to re-evaluate. T. S. Eliot made a selection of Kipling. John Heath-Stubbs has published a selection of Alexander Pope. C. Day Lewis has expressed his admiration of Thomas Hardy in a similar fashion. It is extremely healthy for a young poet, overwhelmed by his admiration of some individual poet, to make up a small selection for himself. He may even find it valuable to add notes, not about the poems' meaning, but about their structures and their most impressive poetic qualities.

Other poets find that it is rejuvenating to tackle the problem of translation. By involving oneself deeply in the sensibility of another poet, and making over that sensibility into one's own words, one can often give one's own poetry a new outlook and a new vitality. Some poets choose to make disciplined and scholarly translations; others prefer to use the original as a source of material for a poem of their own. This is the case with Pound's translations from the Chinese, with the *Imitations* of Robert Lowell, and with Christopher Logue's *Patrocleia*, a superb version of Homer.

A poet must continually stimulate his imagination by all possible means, and he must also continually renew his acquaintance with master-works of the past and present. This is, of course, a way of getting stimulus from outside. He must also, however, be aware of his own private observations and register as much as he can, in actual or mental notes, of his own foibles.

This is perhaps not so easy to describe. Let me, however, use myself as a guinea pig. I have a habit of picking up pebbles and shells on any beach I visit. This is for me, not simply an aesthetic collecting activity but also a pseudo-magical act. I find that I am collecting stones almost as if they were protective amulets. I even, on occasion, find myself talking to them as I select and reject, and when I throw a pebble away it is not a casual act ; it feels like a philosophical or spiritual decision. I am, of course, miming a central aspect of the decision-making and symbol-making elements in living. The psychology of the thing does not, however, concern me. I am only concerned to record this quite commonplace activity and to wonder if I cannot explore my feelings in a poem.

Another writer I know has chosen to record his own intense awareness of the minute details of daily living—his sense that the tablecloth, the dripping water tap, the carpet, the squeaky door, are presences rather than things. In this he is, perhaps, simply repeating something always felt in childhood. He is, however, unashamed of appearing to be childish or childlike. Yet a third writer finds from time to time that his sense of scale becomes distorted ; he sees, as it were, the thrush on the lawn with a worm's eye, as a huge monstrous creature. He finds the salt and pepper pots tower up like cooling towers from the desert of the tablecloth, and he can hold his own house in the palm of his hand. Becoming aware of this at first only occasional oddity of viewpoint, he has capitalized upon it and extended it.

Poets are no different from other people, except in their training themselves to notice all their own sensations. The day-dreamer may transport himself to another country ; the poet will day-dream so much more intensely that he may well feel that other country to be more real than his own. The non-poet of any sensitivity will sometimes question himself as to his own identity. 'Who am I? What am I?', he will ask. What is a momentary depression or passing insecurity in the non-poet is for the poet a more serious matter; he will dwell upon it and live within it until he can, wracked by loss and despair, cry out with Milton's Samson Agonistes 'Dark, dark, dark amid the blaze of noon' or echo the despair of William Cowper at his vision of his own damnation.

The young poet, facing these intensifications of ordinary experience, and these self-dramatizations, may well become extremely troubled and beset by fears. It is, after all, unsettling to wake in the middle of the night with the echo of a voice in your ears, that voice having said something perhaps as odd and yet somehow pregnant as the voice Swift heard :

Midnight Memorandum

Dec. 27, 1733.

I waked at two this morning with the two above lines in my head, which I had made in my sleep, and I wrote them down in the dark, lest I should forget them. But as the original words being writ in the dark, may possibly be mistaken by a careless or unskilful transcriber, I shall give a fairer copy, that two such precious lines may not be lost to posterity:

I walk before no man, a hawk in his fist,
Nor am I a brilliant, whenever I list.

At the very least these moments of intensification cause one to experience, together with that extraordinary sense of clarity, strength, and elation which comes from feeling all one's faculties, including one's intuition, to be at full stretch, a great deal of tension. Human relationships can become distorted and difficult to handle. The wife whose husband is liable, at parties, to get a far-away look in his eye and remain silent in a corner for an hour and a half can become distraught. The parent whose son chooses to spend all one Saturday morning in bed simply *dreaming* may well become fretful. And every family that has a poet to cope with knows that punctuality at meal times is unlikely to be among his virtues. Moreover, the young poet, when a student, is dangerously liable to be obsessed with one aspect of his studies to the detriment of others ; student poets quite frequently have a list of marks that range from an A, let us say in German History, to a D in Victorian Fiction. The poet, indeed, is obliged to follow, as well as he can, a personal discipline that may make other forms of discipline impossible. I say *may* for this is by no means invariable. Many poets are also highly efficient students, scholars, teachers, business men, advertising executives, and private secretaries. Some prefer to avoid responsible positions, however, and live from hand to mouth, or in menial employment, the better to preserve themselves from pressures they have found to be constricting.

Facing these various problems requires a good deal of strength, and tenacity, and also, I fear, a self-confidence that looks uncommonly like arrogance. The arrogance of the poet, however, is not egotistic ; it is rather pride that he has, in some way, been chosen as a vehicle for work for which he can only partially feel responsible. So much of his work is intuitive that he cannot really be conceited about it. He must, however, stick to his conviction that the job is important, and this, again means that he may be resistant to most social pressures.

I have talked about this subject so long because it is important in attempting to discipline oneself into the creation of true poetry, to recognize that poetry involves a life-discipline, and not merely a discipline of the mind. Also, I must point out that, because the poet is so often the outsider, once he feels that his work is not, in fact, good enough to justify his perversities, or once his creative impulse dries up and leaves him feeling he may never again write another poem, he is likely, being a sensitive man, to be wracked with guilt over his selfishness and to feel that his whole life has been wasted in the pursuit of a will o' the wisp. At such times it is hard for anyone to help him. He must help himself.

Dealing with such times of despair and aridity is not easy, but there are methods. The first, and obvious one, is to begin a poetic journal in which one can express one's state of mind. Frequently this leads to a poem, or near-poem, that dramatizes one's condition and thus cures it. Frequently, too, it leads to the realization that what most matters is not the plaudits of the critics but the experience of the vision itself.

The journal, however, doesn't always work. One may, indeed, if one does not catch the problem early enough, find oneself blocked even from writing a journal. One can get over this by making one's comments into a tape recorder. It is the physical act of writing or typing that one is associating with the problem; by being so intensely concerned to write one has made it impossible to do so. The writing has to be of such importance that it is a justification for a lifetime endeavour. No one can write in such circumstances. Therefore one must be cunning; one must produce a substitute for the physical act of writing and yet perform a similarly creative act.

A number of poets, at such times, find it helpful to turn to another art. Many poets paint, or draw. Some make pots. Some are do-it-yourself fiends. As long as one is making something new one is not betraying the poet's conviction, which is that living consists of adding to life rather than in enduring it. To live is to add.

These methods usually work well enough, but there are also others. One is, of course, to get oneself back into the swing of things by parasitic creation and by technical ingenuity. Parasitical creation can take several forms. One kind involves translation—something I have already mentioned. Another exercise is to steal an opening line from another poet's work, for it is often the opening of the poem that presents the most severe block. Typing out a line from another poet (not his opening line, of course, but a line of his that you can see might make a beginning of something else) gets one past the first hurdle. Another technique is to make collage poems as I described them earlier in this book. This avoids that personal justification block; the words are not one's own, therefore personal justification is not involved. Some poets find that, at such times, it is valuable to give poetry readings and thus assure themselves that an audience for their work exists. If the audience is receptive, then a little of the pressure is off. On the other hand, if one is a good performer the very applause one receives may strike one as being applause for a dead self and thus increase one's sense of desolation.

Most poets, however, have purely personal release strategies. One poet I know finds that he can get rid of the build-up of tension by listening to a particular piece of music on his record player. He never plays this music except in connection with his writing. One can, indeed, build up conditioned reflexes for oneself. If one has, usually by an accident of circumstances, always written poetry at a particular desk, then that desk itself may stimulate one into writing. One can, however, get hooked on these symbolic objects or environments. It is said that Pierre Jean-Jouve, leaving Paris for the country, was obliged always to take with him the chair in which he wrote his poems. Many poets find they can only write in pencil, or on their own typewriters, or in penny notebooks, or on pink paper. A good many poets, of course, find that if they reduce sexual tension by making love to a new girl, they assure themselves of their own physical attractiveness and potency, and, by a kind of psychological analogy, convince themselves of their poetic vitality and power. Others find that getting drunk helps, not so much because of the drunken exuberance itself, but because the lowered vitality of the following day is accompanied by a vagueness of mind and a dreaminess that can be exploited, in order to get down, not perhaps a poem, but the beginnings of one.

Dealing with total blockage is, however, often easier than dealing with a sense of staleness. One has, let us say, been writing fairly steadily for some months, and then one discovers that one has begun to repeat oneself, and that the new poems are both highly predictable and dreadfully dull. It is at this point that one must take action. Most poets are so aware of the danger of self-imitation and of becoming gimmicky that they distrust those poems they have written which turn out to be popular, being afraid that their natural human love of praise will lead them to work towards easy success. How can one deal with this situation?

Again, non-writing, free-association exercises, and a poetic journal may help. They may not, however, provide enough novel material to produce creative tensions. If this is the case it is often useful to set oneself a task that is intellectually interesting enough to produce a kind of excitement, and absurd enough to return one to a condition of irresponsibility. One such exercise is to challenge poetic conventions in one way or another. Attempt to write a poem without any adjectives. This gives one a totally new slant on one's own vocabulary, and forces one to gain a new, and stimulating, perspective upon language. If this does not appeal, try a hitherto untried verse form, or deliberately choose a subject that seems novel and see how many poetic notes you can make about it. Poets are often great readers of diaries, biographies, and travel books; these will, sometimes, enable you to challenge yourself with a task. One might, for example, choose to write a sequence of poems based upon events in the life of some fascinating saint or sinner. One might write a travel sequence based upon the journal of a voyage of exploration. It does not really matter what one attempts as long as it is novel and one is aware that there is a sporting chance of complete failure.

This may sound absurd, but one must remember that poetry is an exploration, an adventure. One needs, therefore, at times of staleness to give oneself the stimulus of insecurity. There is, it seems, an adrenalin of the imagination, which will respond to insecurity as does the adrenalin of the physical body. But one must be careful to challenge oneself with something that seems at least reasonably important, or technically a true challenge. Simply choosing to write in one's old stale manner about new subject matter is no solution. One should try to adventure in both subject matter and style.

There are a number of other, minor, challenges one can give oneself at moments of hesitation and dullness. One is to start a poem *in medias res*, in the middle of some unknown (because as yet unimagined) event or action. One might, for example, start off:

> and then he ran up the hillside
> scattering stones
> behind him in an avalanche . . .

This must be followed through as one follows a daydream, letting a pattern emerge.

> I turned
> to her, and took her hand.
> Had he gone mad,
> or were we, in our . . .

The *in medias res* opening need not, of course, suggest narrative. It may, for example, be:

> . . . Which has been said before . . .

And, possibly, lead on to:

> so many times,
> but never with such bitterness.

Now we clearly need some proverb or cliché, and that will give the poem a theme to elaborate, or suggest a human situation to explore.

There is a game much played by poets which has never been given a name, but which I will call *The Title Game*. It consists of taking up a phrase or statement someone has just produced in casual conversation and adding to it the words *and Other Poems*. This can have comic results, for it often results in a near-parody of existing book titles. But the game shows, quite surprisingly, just how many casual unforced phrases can be accepted as credible poem titles or first lines. Consider the following dull exchange:

> How do you feel ?
> Fine, thanks. Just back from a visit to Vegas.
> Did you end up winning ?
> Not on your life! Does anybody!
> I guess some do. I never did.

I can easily believe in *How do you feel, and Other Poems*. It could be a sardonic, rather disturbing collection with philosophical overtones. *A Visit to Vegas and Other Poems* is a rather tiresome book of poems about places, I fear. On the other hand *Not On Your Life and Other Poems* sounds somewhat challenging while *I guess Some Do and Other Poems* has a pleasingly enigmatic quality and hints, I feel, at one of those laconic, witty, rather sour volumes. Of course, there are variants of this game; one can add to the phrase *Starring Theda Bara* or some such name and turn it into a picture, or one can give it a subtitle. *A Visit to Vegas* might be subtitled *or The Loss of The Titanic*. Such verbal games point to the way in which the most commonplace expression, if taken from its context, and given emphasis, can lead one to perceive imaginative possibilities. One poet I know has in his notebooks a whole series of such phrases. There are road signs: *Soft Shoulders, Slippery when wet, Beware of the Sheep*. There are clichés: *Terribly clever, Flying High, Bottoms up*; there are snatches of overheard conversation.

Such notes may not lead to poems. The words noted down may never become part of any piece of writing. Their function is more to keep one on the *qui vive* and to remind one that an ordinary event can be seen as significant and symbolic if one chooses to look at it sideways.

This sideways looking requires practice, of course. Mostly it consists of taking phenomena out of context and seeing what they, by themselves, contain that is useful or mysterious or significant. Abstract, for example, from your vision of a kitchen, all the knives that are lying around, and you will see the kitchen as a sacrificial place and relate it, as many have done in the past, to religious feelings and to sacramental observances. Observe in the nursery the battered doll or teddy bear and you may find yourself writing a poem like Thomas Kinsella's *Soft Toy*.

Soft Toy

I am soiled with the repetition of your loves and hatreds
  And other experiments. You do not hate me,
Crumpled in my corner. You do not love me,
  A small heaped corpse. My face of beaten fur
Responds as you please: if you do not smile
  It does not smile; to impatience or distaste
It answers blankness, beyond your goodwill
  —Blank conviction, beyond your understanding or mine.

I lie limp with use and re-use, listening.
  Loose ends of conversations, hesitations,
Half-beginnings, that peter out in my presence,
  Are enough. I understand, with a flame of shame
Or a click of ease or joy, inert. Knowledge
  Into resignation: the process drives deeper,
Grows clearer, eradicating chance growths of desire
  —And colder: all possibilities of desire.

My button-brown hard eyes fix on your need
  To grow, as you crush me with tears and throw me aside.
Most they reflect, but something absorb—brightening
  In response, with energy, to the energy of your changes.

Clutched tightly through the night, held before you,
   Ragged and quietly crumpled, as you thrust, are thrust,
In dull terror into your opening brain,
   I face the dark with eyes that cannot close
—The cold, outermost points of your will, as you sleep.
   Between your tyrannous pressure and the black
Resistance of the void my blankness hardens
   To a blunt probe, a cold pitted grey face.

The creation of such poetry demands that one observes continually and minutely. It also means, however, that one's vision must be selective. It is interesting to go in a group to a particular place or event and to write down, severally, the most interesting and provocative images. While there is always a degree of agreement, there are also, always, differences. A poet in a fairground may easily find himself paying more attention to the crumpled papers upon the ground than to the carousel or roller-coaster. Another may find himself obsessed with the model ducks that swim by in the shooting gallery, while a third may perceive symbolic possibilities in the coin-rolling stall.

Selective vision implies, of course, partial blindness, and practising poets are among the most noticing and the most oblivious people I know. They tend to discount the obvious elements of phenomena, and concentrate upon minutiae. They may not recall the name of a place, but they will remember an old man they saw there who had a black dog on a piece of string. They may forget a person's name, but remember his gold tooth or small ear lobes. They are at once the most and the least attentive listeners. They listen intensely until something usable is said, or something that deserves a little exploration; then they switch off their attention.

Of course, no one person is the same as another, and there are many poets who reveal few eccentricities, and appear to run their lives in as orderly and even predictable manner as anyone else. This is, however, invariably only a surface appearance. One cannot practise poetry seriously without adjusting one's life to the demands it makes, and these demands are so continuous and so considerable as to produce effects which may seem to others to be rather odd, though they are, surely, no more odd than the effects produced by the demands of other professions, or other trades. The only difference is that the poet, like the policeman, perhaps, or the priest, or the journalist, or, certainly, the painter and sculptor, is never completely off duty, and what is least noticed by others is likely to be that to which he finds himself paying most attention. Consider, for example, junk. Here is a poem by Tony Connor which is really about poetry itself, about the necessity of observing, using, revering even, those aspects of life which we all tend to ignore, discard, or desire.

Considering Junk

It lies there, vivid in its dereliction,
among fine ashes from combustion stoves,
drippings of tinned tomatoes
that smelled peculiar, soiled disposable
nappies, and other household grot.

Having exhausted, or frustrated, expectation,
It emanates a certain smugness—
if you are of such a mind to think so.

A painter might take away the slither
of red polythene down a scorched bucket
into the crumbly texture of old flock
beneath: a sculptor—to the point of plundering—
broken bannister-ends like totems
to an ultimate, perfect, mass beyond masses.

You may look at it in different ways . . .

There are, for instance, certainly, numerous
homilies here for the religious man
with a touch of the poet.
        As for the poet
himself; in this rigorous age he is wary of metaphor,
far more of symbol, and if he is the householder
(as I am) whose annual clear-out
has overflowed dustbin, grocery-boxes,
and mildewed, split trunk, onto
the garden path, his dreams alone are likely
to dwell on things he threw away.
        Cumbersome, brokendown
junk talking all night with the eloquence of poems.

Here the poet, wary of easy rhetoric and pretentious symbolism never-theless finds himself making symbols, and unable to avoid expressing reverence for discarded hoped and ruined beliefs. The poet is, indeed, a man possessed. If one is not possessed by a sense of the overriding im-portance of making poems; if one is not compelled to make them, and if one does not discipline one's life in terms of poetry, then one is not, perhaps a poet, though one may make poems and some of them may be good.

There is nothing wrong with being a maker of poems rather than a poet. There is, indeed, much to be said for it, and many of our finest works have been created by such people. Nevertheless, there comes a point in one's pursuit of the practice of poetry when one has to decide whether or not one wishes to commit oneself wholeheartedly to this vocation. One has, perhaps, to decide whether enough of one's poems have been compulsive, and enough of one's visions unasked for and astonishing, for one to judge that one is, of necessity, obliged to go on as a poet. Of course, the decision is usually made unconsciously. One's own way of life will make the decision. Nevertheless, it is one that, sooner or later, must be made, and made not by the mind, but by the whole personality.

EIGHT Strategies and Programmes

The concept of genre, which I touched on in an earlier chapter, is less important, today, perhaps than it has been in the past. For the practising poet, it is of less crucial importance than to the literary historian, who is happy to point out, for example, that in the seventeenth century the pastoral genre almost invariably involved certain kinds of imagery and certain types of allusion, while in the eighteenth century these altered. Nevertheless, the practising poet does need to consider, when he is revising the first draft of his poem, whether or not it belongs to any definable genre. If he does not know that, in the past, the satire or the elegy or the pastoral or the ballad, have had certain characteristics, he cannot capitalize upon those characteristics by either imitating them or countering them. A man attempting an elegy would be a fool if he did not have in his mind Milton's *Lycidas* or Grey's *Elegy*. A poet writing satire would be stupid not to have at the back of his mind the satires of John Skelton, Pope, Swift, Churchill, and Byron, and perhaps the later ones of W. H. Auden and Roy Campbell. When attempting an Eclogue, the poet should know of the conventional classical eclogue as imitated in the seventeenth and eighteenth centuries; he should also know Louis MacNeice's *Eclogue by a five barred Gate,* and some of the dialogue poems of Hardy and Auden.

It is not my purpose to write an analysis of the different genres here, but merely to indicate that awareness of them is essential. In most cases there are genre-anthologies available—collections of satire, and of ballads—and there are enough critical works on the epic to direct one's attention to the most useful texts.

It is, however, likely that the young poet will not, in the twentieth century, write in definable genres unless he has a profound interest in traditional attitudes. For the most part he will write poems from a position he feels to be, if not unique, at least individual. In so doing, however, he must, as Eliot has pointed out, be aware of other poets who have tackled similar problems or written from similar viewpoints. His poem is, after all, only truly original if it adds to, or develops in some way the total achievement of the poetry of a particular kind. It is, for example, necessary, if one is writing a Dramatic Monologue to ask oneself if one is doing or saying anything that has not been already better done or said by Browning, Eliot, Robert Frost, and a host of others. If one is writing a ballad one must consider, not only the folk ballads of the past, the border ballads and the ballads of the Appalachians, but also the more recent uses of the form by W. H. Auden, Charles Causley, W. S. Graham, John Betjeman, and W. B. Yeats—again to mention only a few.

This approach to poetry is, of course, not that of the historian, for the historian does not tend, usually, to think in genre-terms except as connected with the sensibility of a given or of succeeding periods. Moreover, the historian tends to think of poet A influencing poet B, whereas, quite frequently, it is a case of Poets A and B simply tackling a similar problem. Moreover, poets tend to cross genre-lines rather frequently. They are likely to ask, for example, 'What if I use the rhythm of a hymn to write a satire?' (It has been done.) They may wonder what would happen if they tackled a description of urban industrial landscape in a diction appropriate to idealistic pastoral. (It's been done.) They may even, perceiving a poetic strategy in an epic passage, choose to use that same strategy in a poem of an entirely different tone. Indeed, one of the things one must learn to do is to ask continually, *What if?* and suggest to oneself new combinations and permutations of existing approaches and techniques.

Sooner or later, however, the young poet finds himself, consciously, or unconsciously, with a *programme* and with a conviction that, for him, the real heart of poetry lies in some particular and limited approach. He works, one might say, with a limited range of colours on his palette. The history of poetry is filled with such theories. Some were peculiar to individual poets, and some to schools or movements. Sometimes they occur as a result of poets gathering together and finding common interests, as happened with the Surrealist Movement in France, and sometimes a journalist commentator, perceiving similarities in the work of a number of poets invents a school. This happened in the 1950s in England when an article in *The Spectator* suggested the existence of a New Movement in English writing, and duly identified those poets and novelists who belonged to it. In America at the moment some feel there is a Confessional School, the members of which make their poems from autobiographical material of a disturbingly intimate kind. Anne Sexton and Robert Lowell are, supposedly, leaders of this school, but, in reality, it exists more in the minds of the critics than in the minds of the poets. It is simply that Lowell brought into poetry a new type of dramatic monologue making apparent use of confessional material, and that poets have seized upon this new approach with enthusiasm. It is another poetic strategy.

I have used the word *strategy* several times, and must now say what I mean by the term. Basically a *poetic strategy* is, like a poetic plot, a formula for achieving certain effects. It can be attached to notions of subject matter, or diction, or rhyme or metre, but usually it refers to the overall organization of a poem. Poets who invent new strategies are commonly regarded with admiration by their peers, and are frequently imitated. It was the discovery of a new strategy by Wordsworth which was influential, not his nature-worship, or his poetic language, or his reaction against the high poetic diction of some of his forebears. It was Pope's strategy that brought him followers, and his control of the heroic couplet was only one aspect of that strategy. When Theodore Roethke discovered the strategy of getting inside a child's mind by recording a series of fragmentary but vivid perceptions in simple language, and avoiding any kind of overt explanation, he created a strategy which other poets immediately saw to be useful. And when Milton created that extraordinary latinate diction for *Paradise Lost* it was part of an overall strategy to control the audience's response to his message.

One must make a distinction between a poet's *strategy* and his *programme*. They may be very much involved with one another, but the one is not always an explanation of the other. When Poe, in his extraordinary essay on the writing of *The Raven* attempted to describe how he planned and got his effects, he was displaying a strategy. When Wordsworth wrote his *Preface to the Lyrical Ballads* he was outlining a programme that did not, in fact, at any point really mention the nature of his strategic discoveries.

One type of strategy involves the creation of a deliberately peculiar approach to phenomena, one that requires the reader to make a special effort of sympathy in order to share the poem's perceptions. Walter de la Mare made use of this kind of strategy in many of his poems. A good example is *The Song of the Mad Prince*.

> Who said 'Peacock Pie'?
>   The old King to the sparrow:
> Who said, 'Crops are ripe'?
>   Rust to the harrow:

Who said, 'Where sleeps she now?
  Where rests she now her head,
Bathed in eve's loveliness'?
  That's what I said.

Who said, 'Ay, mum's the word';
  Sexton to willow:
Who said, 'Green dusk for dreams,
  Moss for a pillow'?
Who said, 'All Time's delight
  Hath she for narrow bed;
Life's troubled bubble broken'?—
  That's what I said.

The Song of the Mad Prince was included in de la Mare's 1944 collection, *Collected Rhymes and Verses*. In the preface to this book, in which he gathered together the contents of a number of volumes, he stated 'most of the volumes here referred to were intended for children.' Like many of de la Mare's poems, however, this particular piece is using childhood, the child-mind, as a means of exploring the adult one. While the first two lines may suggest an allusion to a fairy tale, and the two following lines some fable for children, the next four lines are, neither in diction nor in message, particularly appropriate to a children's story. When we move into the second stanza the first two lines, though paralleling the construction of the opening of the previous stanza, relate less to nursery literature than to folk literature and suggest the world of ballads rather than that of Perrault or the simplified versions of the Grimm Brothers.

The poem makes use, too, of the enigma in a highly sophisticated fashion. We are required to guess at the significance of the questions and answers. Why did the King say *Peacock pie* to the sparrow? It may be that he was pointing out that the peacocks, the proud, in this world are those who attract predators, and that humility and lowliness are often protections against the appetites of the powerful greedy and the sensation-seekers. The statement *Crops are ripe* is a little easier to understand, for it derives simply from the assumption that the rust is aware of the passing of the seasons. But just as *peacock pie* suggests death, so does the reference to rust, for after the harvest the harrow must be cleaned for use. Therefore, though the next question seems at first to be unconnected to the earlier ones, it does in fact take up the theme of death, in that one answer to both questions posed could clearly involve death.

The death theme only emerges clearly, however, with the introduction of the sexton (who buries the dead) and the willow, which is a tree of mourning. The greenness we associate with trees, and with willows therefore, emerges as an explicit reference now. We suspect the green dusk refers to the sleep of dreams mentioned by Hamlet, and the phrase *moss for a pillow* reinforces our impression. The phrase *narrow bed* makes the grave theme even more clear, and the theme itself becomes explicit with the phrase: *life's troubled bubble broken.*

The strategy, therefore, is to pose questions which, together with their answers, move from being hard to explain to being easy, and which all involve a possible allusion to death. The title suggests that the childlikeness of part of the poem derives from madness, and, as the poem proceeds, we may even suspect a particular madness and a particular death are involved. It is Ophelia who had a prince for a suitor, and who died singing, drifting downstream under the willows. Ophelia, too, refers to willows in her madness, and the queen describes her death as attended by bubbles. This is, therefore, a lament for, if not Ophelia, a girl who has committed suicide.

Looking back over the poem now one can see that the *peacock pie* may refer to the suffering a person may bring on himself or herself by attracting the attention and the desire of others. The statement of the rust to the harrow becomes now much more savage as the word *ripe* takes on a possible sexual meaning. Moreover, the *rust*, the image of long neglect and decay, is speaking to the *harrow*, the image of destruction, of the earth being clawed. The harrow is, like the King, old, and has been neglected since the sowing of the seed. Now it can rejoice in the suffering of the land again that has escaped its attentions for so long. If we think of the play of *Hamlet* we may remember Claudius sicking Ophelia onto Hamlet, saying, in effect, that she is *ripe.* If we do go this far, however, we are turning the poem into an allegory, which it is not. But we are surely right in seeing the Hamlet–Ophelia situation behind the song.

The strategy is what concerns us, however. It is basically a strategy of linked enigmas, and therefore it is dependent upon our being curious about meanings. The connection between the parts of the poem is suggested by parallelism of construction. The theme emerges only gradually into the light. This type of strategy involves, essentially, the use of associative leaps and of those richly vivid fantasies we connect with childhood, with emotional disturbance, and with drama.

H. R. Hays' poem *Housing Development* also makes use of the fantastic. Here, however, the strategy is to translate the commonplace coherence of an urban housing development into terms of the phenomena one associates with conventional bourgeois life, and so to arrange these phenomena that they make no logical pattern, but rather a succession of vivid and disjointed perceptions. Thus the hallucinatory liveliness of the imagery acts as a counterpoint to the commonplace setting, and reminds us—which is the intention of the poem—that, in reality, there is no aspect of life untouched by human pain and by the human yearning after the dramatic and ideal.

> Their eyes are full of newspapers
> Stealthily the carpet
> Creeps from wall to wall.
> They button on roast chickens,
> Make hats of armchairs
> And fold whisky and water into each napkin.
>
> If you plant a wedding cake on the lawn
> Will it grow baby pictures?
> Will it sing 'My country 'tis of thee?'
>
> Imagine the screams
> If a mermaid appeared in the bathtub,
> The distress of the vacuum cleaner,
> The soapy sobs of the dishwasher.
>
> Fortunately there are no tears
> In the salad,
> Only a life insurance policy
> Garnished with walnuts.
>
> And yet
> All along the block
> Breasts peer out of windows
> And from the television antennae
> Drops of blood fall.

Surrealist poetry is, of course, a complicated subject to discuss. Hays' poem, however, is a useful illustration of the general principle that if you, in observing a commonplace scene, select the least commonplace images and juxtapose them for surprise-effects, you can imply something important about the way in which our visions of reality are governed by our viewpoints. We make our own world; we are inextricably part, and author, of the world we regard as external to ourselves.

Poetic strategies of this kind necessarily involve a philosophical attitude. They suggest a world-view. This is even true of such strategies as that superbly simple one used by John Knight in his *Poem of the Fancy*. Here the title appears to dismiss the poem as a slight production of slight importance. The poem itself, also, is written in a casual, almost prosy manner, and the wit involved in seeing the old man grow younger rather than older as time passes seems also to be rather an easy device at first. The last two lines, however, have force and philosophical intent, and the word *Fancy* in the title now appears ironic. The whole tone of the poem suggests an overall attitude, a world-view, and the poem itself is in part intended not to make a particular point but to oblige us, for a time, to examine our life from a new angle.

> The first time I saw Death he was an old man;
>   nine hundred and sixty-nine they said, I think.
>
> Next time I saw him there were red hairs among the grey;
>   time makes its mark, they said.
>
> When he taught us at school we showed him little respect,
>   considering his decreasing years.
>
> Last time I ran across him I noticed how much he'd unaged;
>   he noticed me, too, and nodded.
>
> His acquaintance, they say, turns in time to friendship;
>   but that's as may be, I say.
>
> I think that, after the usual formalities,
>   young Death will quickly forget.

Basically the strategies I have described are ways of establishing a particularity of viewpoint, and of suggesting a distorting mirror through which the world appears in a different disguise. Many poets use the same mirror over and over again, and thus one finds oneself speaking of the *Thought* of X, or the *Message* of the poetry of Y. Frequently a poet discovers a particular strategy to suit him so well, and to fit so well with his actual beliefs that he mounts a real programme and continues to develop ways of presenting his approach. Of course, some poets operate from the opposite point of view; filled with a philosophical conviction and desirous of spreading their gospel they hunt for strategies appropriate to their philosophies. It is, however, usually fair to say that the new programme of a poet derives always in part from technical excitements and strategic experiments, and rarely wholly from intellectual convictions.

One cannot, perhaps, by will, create either new programmes or new strategies. One can only watch the way one's work develops, and then rationalize about it and develop new approaches. But it might be useful to illustrate just how a poet can develop a strategy, by indulging again in a little self-commentary.

In 1963, on my return to London from teaching in the U.S.A. and at the University of Victoria on Vancouver Island, I met a man in a pub called Frank Fryett. In conversation I discovered that he too knew Vancouver Island, and had in fact been repatriated there after the Second World War. He had been a Japanese prisoner-of-war and was working down a mine near Nagasaki when the bomb fell; he was marched through the ruins of Nagasaki to his ship and sent to a rehabilitation centre at Esquimalt, near Victoria.

This story struck me forcibly. Here was I, having just left Esquimalt and Victoria with a clear picture of them in my mind. And here was another man with an equally clear, but different picture of the same place. The past and present became interwoven in my mind and I wrote a poem in which I attempted to place past and present alongside one another.

> *Remembering Esquimalt*
>
> *For Frank Fryett, who, after several years in a Japanese Prisoner of War Camp near Nagasaki, was repatriated to a Rehabilitation Centre at Esquimalt on Vancouver Island*
>
> For rehabilitation
> his camp was Esquimalt.
> I remembered the kelp
> in the tangling sea,
> and the English gardens;
> he remembered snow,
> and eating meat, and
> walking alone at night,
>
> those years ago. V.J. Day
> he'd seen a mirror.
> 'Christ,' he said, 'I'm
> bent as a bloody crone!'
> 'You've had that crook back
> all the bloody time
> we've been in the mine!' they said:
> he hadn't known.

And marching through Nagasaki,
'It looked like a flower
among the stones,' he said,
'a cup and saucer
melted and hardened back
into folds of petals.
Lovely it was,' he said,
'but I felt sick

thinking about it after.'
We drank to Esquimalt,
all that clean blue air.
'One day,' he said,
'on the ship from Java
we saw a tanker struck,
and the bastards burning and
running about like mad

ants, all burning whether
they jumped or not.
The sea was on fire,' he said.
'We laughed and clapped
and cheered and stamped
to see the buggers trapped.
It isn't nice to think of
the way you get,

or even some things you've seen.
I liked Esquimalt.
They asked us to dances.'
He picked up his stick.
'A bit like a rose,' he said,
'I should have kept it.
That was one of the things
I should have kept.'

This poem was written together with others using a similar juxtaposition of the present and the past during the spring of 1963. It had, however, been anticipated by a number of other poems written at the University of Massachusetts in October–December, 1962. I was, in fact, on the point of moving permanently away from England, and found myself therefore looking back at the past and seeing it alongside the present in a series of poems.

The strategy here only became really apparent to me, however, when I realized that while all these poems were about the way memories disturbed the present, the basic technique was to *plait* two themes together, to alternate two stories or two viewpoints that appeared at first to be quite distinct from one another. I realized that the seed of this type of strategy lay in Browning's dramatic monologues, especially in *Fra Lippo Lippi*, and in some of the poems of Wordsworth. I began, however, to wonder if the formula could be applied without the use of an auto-biographical or pseudo-autobiographical approach.

It was shortly after the death of Theodore Roethke in July, 1963 that I found a theme which enabled me to try the strategy again. Mrs. Roethke gave me her late husband's shirts as I was one of the few friends large enough to wear them. At about the same time I read the story of Wovoka, the Paiute Indian, and the Ghost Dance War. Wovoka gave his followers special shirts which, he said, made them impervious to the bullets of the white man. Unfortunately they proved ineffective. The connection between Wovoka's shirts and Theodore Roethke's shirts seemed purely verbal, but I began a poem in which I alternated the two references to see what would happen. I called the poem *Ghost Shirts*.

> Wovoka believed
> in a Messiah,
> a newcomer,
> the plains black
> with buffalo,
> taught the tribes to dance,
> tell the truth,
> not fear death,
> and gave them shirts.
> This morning shirts
> arrive for me
> from a dead poet.
>
> Imagination
> evolves death.
> They sang through bullets,
> boys in rain
> catching the wet in their
> mouths, licking
> their bare arms.
> The shirt fits;
> the same shoulders,
> the same neck:
> I stare out from
> his photograph.

The consequences
of prophecy matter
less than the act.
At Wounded Knee
that Christmas time
two hundred died;
for thirty days
the Ghost Dance War
choked up the trails.
The Gods allow
us transformations
the earth foils.

I wear a dead poet's
shirt. Belief
derides the ring of
firelit faces,
as all history;
in Nevada
the prophet,
every victory won,
praised as I praise
the dead that dance
the dance are truthful,
and consume.

Now the conclusion of this poem is hardly very original, but it has been qualified by the preceding lines so that sympathy for and awe at the faith of the poet and at the faith of the martyr are fused together. The poem is thus not about my wearing a great poet's shirt as if I believed it might protect or inspire me; nor is it about the wearing of holy shirts by Wovoka's braves. It is about a human impulse towards faith that is so strong that it can lead to happy and confident martyrdom; hence the reference to the *ring of firelit faces* around the stake at which some martyr (Joan of Arc ? Latimer ?) is being burned.

The plaiting strategy involved here is easy enough to practise once it has been identified. I myself have used it a number of times though at the time of writing I feel I have got all the mileage out of it that I can, at least for the present, and am now trying out other approaches. Some of these are deliberately planned. Some have developed and are developing out of purely intuitional discoveries and explorations.

Were I another kind of man, I might, of course suggest that the proper thing for poetry to do nowadays would be to juxtapose apparently disparate stories or elements in this manner. I might argue that a divided world demands a poetry in which divisions are fused into unity; I might even suggest that the plaited poem serves as a kind of moral example to all readers of the way in which life must be brought into unity, and all tensions healed. It would be a bad programme, and a silly and pretentious one, though there have been others just as silly which have commanded followings in the past.

The only programme I can give myself, however, and the only one most poets give themselves, is to follow up my own chance discoveries, to study new possibilities of strategy, and to leave as few possibilities untried as possible. Some poets, however, usually in their middle years find that, upon reflection, all their work and all their studies have bred in them a conviction which provides a poetic philosophy that they must recognize, explain, and follow. Two poets of the twentieth century have written books about their own systems of thought. In 1925 W. B. Yeats published his *A Vision* and in 1947 Robert Graves issued his *The White Goddess*. These systems are not valid for most other poets, but they repay attention. One way in which to discover for oneself, if not a whole poetic philosophy, then, at least, a series of productive attitudes, is to study those books in which poets have attempted to come to grips with the nature of their imagination and poetic faculty. The great grandfather of such works is, of course, Coleridge's *Biographia Literaria*, but there are many others.

Such philosophical systems provide a poet with a framework in which he can place his poems, and also indicate further subjects and approaches to him. Religious beliefs can, of course, be equally helpful in this regard, though the belief in a religious creed is always liable to cause the poet to prize his spiritual message above his poetic efficiency, and even to distort the vision of a poem in the service of a particular belief. Whether or not this is a good thing to do is a matter upon which there may be some disagreement. My own purely personal view is that the practice of poetry itself constitutes a faith and a belief and that I cannot afford to endanger it by accepting other orthodoxies. Robert Graves also takes this point of view, but it is only fair to point out that other poets of our time, notably T. S. Eliot and W. H. Auden, have found orthodox Christianity acceptable.

This may seem a digression. It is, however, leading to the point that the practising poet will find himself obliged to concern himself with theology, philosophy, anthropology, and psychology as well as with purely literary matters. The source material of poetry must always be that which has most disturbed the emotions and excited the speculations of men. Moreover, by exploring the beliefs, customs, and symbols of others, the young poet will enlarge the range of his sympathies and gain new perspectives upon his own limited experience.

It cannot be said too emphatically that the practising poet is unlikely to be more than an amateur in these fields. Indeed, he is almost required to retain his amateur status, for he is obliged to use the discoveries of the anthropologist and the philosopher as material for entirely poetic speculations, and these may well lead to views which the original authorities would find somewhat odd. Perhaps anthropology and mythology are the two most useful sources of poetry. While it is no longer fashionable to lard one's verse with mythological references, an understanding of the themes and beliefs which recur in mythologies of all nations can give a poet a hint as to what is most basic to the human imagination. He may choose to believe, with Jung, that stories which crop up in all cultures are archetypal and describe matters basic to the human psyche. Whether or not Jung is correct, the poet may well find it useful to adopt this view. He may, for example, in reading the legend of Leda and the Swan see it, as Yeats saw it, as a symbol of possession of the human consciousness by some other will, or other intelligence. He may relate it indeed to those times when he himself, working intuitively, feels as if possessed by another mind and sensibility, or as if dictated to by some other voice.

If one wishes to suggest the ways in which the poet may learn to handle this material one is, perhaps, reduced to exercises which sound naïve. Let us, however, assume that we have just read a page or two of Smith's *Shorter Classical Dictionary*, and have come across the myth of Sysyphus who was condemned to roll a boulder up a hill in Hades only to have it roll down again, crushing him in its path on each occasion. This is so obvious an illustration of both stubbornness and frustration that one may think to use it. How? I would suggest that one might outline another type of unavailing struggle and give it universal significance by alluding, briefly, to Sysyphus, or by querying whether or not the place in which such frustration always occurs is probably hell, a place of torment, a place of damnation. Are we all Sysyphus?

Trite though this may appear, the technique it illustrates is valuable. Mythological references can universalize the slightest of anecdotes and give them symbolic power with very little effort or verbiage.

Mythology, however, often enables one to look at ordinary emotional crises with new eyes. The soldier and his girl friends, for example—can they be versions, echoes in our time as it were, of Mars and Venus? Or perhaps one can reverse this process and write a poem about the love of Mars for Venus by treating them as if they were twentieth-century people, exploring myth as if it were actuality.

The study of anthropology, especially the old-fashioned anthropology of Frazer in *The Golden Bough*, yields many interesting and sometimes bizarre customs for scrutiny, and for possible juxtaposition with day-to-day events. The animal worshippers for example; can we not see the old lady with her fat Pekinese as in some way paying tribute still to an animal god? Can we not understand the witch and her familiar to have been reborn in the man and his dog, the spinster and her budgerigar? Isn't there a theme here somewhere?

Psychology is less obviously productive, though here one can find—especially in the books of Jung and Freud—many dream histories and many analyses of symbols which may suggest fruitful jungles to explore. In case histories one can find themes for speculation. What about the man Antephoron mentioned by Burton in his *Anatomy of Melancholy* who 'saw always before him his own face as in a glass'? Is not this an image of self-absorption neatly dramatized ready for us. I thought so when I first came across it and I included a poem called *Antephoron* in my first book.

Theology is, perhaps, less vital to the poet than hagiography. The saints and martyrs, like the heroes and gods of Greece and Rome, often led rather odd lives, and their visions and agonies often pattern, in large scale, the small-scale disturbances and confrontations of our own. Again, it is not always wise to allude; it is often better simply to take the suggested theme. Sometimes of course one may produce a dramatic monologue or poem about a specific saint, as did Tennyson with St. Simon Stylites, and as did Wilde with St. Sebastian.

I often suggest to my students that they try to rewrite, in their own colloquial modern voices, the story of a myth or a saint. The use of modern speech for ancient themes can not only revive those themes and bring them home to us again; it can also suggest the difference between the modern and the ancient sensibility. Thom Gunn wrote a poem about Saint Martin which does just this, and there have been many modern retellings of biblical stories, perhaps the most notable being T. S. Eliot's *Journey of the Magi*.

Such tasks as these are, however, only of value when the poet himself is not involved in explorations of his own. It must be emphasized over and over again that the practice of poetry is a process of self-discovery and of seeking for hidden truths. No man can teach another to be a poet as distinct from a writer of poems. That is a matter of personal commitment, and very few of the millions of would-be poets and accomplished writers of poems are likely to take that last step.

NINE The Final Commitment

We have now reached the point where there is little else that can be said about the practice of poetry without going into subtleties and complexities inappropriate to this particular book. Everything I have touched on, however briefly, could easily be used as material for a book in itself, and, of course, many books have been written on these matters, though astonishingly few have been written from the viewpoint of the practising poet, as distinguished from the literary historian or the prosodist. I have attempted only to sketch briefly a number of approaches to the practice of poetry, in the hope that these may prove of use to would-be poets and to teachers. Finally, however, I must mention the most important factor in the writing of poetry, for this is the individual's own unique involvement in the act of living and his own unique pattern of compulsion and cunning.

Here we are upon slippery ground. Poetry is a vocation as priesthood is, or should be, a vocation. Many people serve their church with dedication, but only the priest lives, or should live, entirely in terms of that dedication. So it is with the poet as distinct from the poem-writer. The poet, however, unlike the priest, has no supporting organization. His life is, moreover, dedicated to beliefs and practices which do little to provide him with an income, and he must, therefore, be absolutely determined to devote himself to poetry if he is not to fail in his purpose because of economic pressures and the demands made upon him by his more remunerative work. Each poet will find a different solution to this problem. Some choose to earn their money in work so remote from poetry as to provide no opportunity for their psychic energies to be misapplied. Others contrive, by becoming teachers of Creative Writing, or Poets in Residence at Universities, to serve poetry in more than one manner. Some, of course, choose a life of poverty, or of bohemian carelessness. In every case, however, it is clear that the life must be adjusted to the demands of poetry and not vice versa.

There is, however, another difficulty here. Some poem-writers of ability regard themselves as poets and attempt to live as poets in a state of continual dedication. If they are not true poets the result is often unpleasant. The poems cease to be good; the vision fails; and the poem-writer finds himself a despised and ridiculed figure unable to escape from his remunerative role as Professor or Poet in Residence, or psychologically unable to change a way of life that now no longer can be justified even by himself. The American novelist George Cuomo told me once that whenever a young writer asked him, 'Shall I go on writing?' he answered, 'No', in the well-founded belief that if the question was in any way a serious enquiry the young writer could not be possessed by that true sense of compulsion, by that relentless drive, which alone will result in work that can justify the dedication and suffering involved.

It is no longer fashionable to regard the poet as a lonely and dedicated figure. There are many competent and even brilliant poem-writers who maintain that poetry can be an occasional occupation, and I have myself heard several critics and editors say that they used to write poetry but now no longer have the time. They may, they say, write poetry again. They could, of course, if they wished. Their tone is superior, and their insecurity obvious. Poetry, to them, is no more than a pastime.

Poetry is not, however, a game, though game-playing is often involved in it. Poetry is a way of life. There is a passage by Rainer Maria Rilke which should be given to every would-be poet to read. Rilke said:

> You ask if your verses are good. You ask me. You have previously asked others. You send them to journals. You compare them with other poems, and you are troubled when certain editors reject your efforts. Now (as you have permitted me to advise you) I beg you to give all that up. You are looking outwards, and of all things that is what you must now not do. Nobody can advise and help you, nobody. There is only one single means. Go inside yourself. Discover the motive that bids you write; examine whether it sends its roots down to the deepest places of your heart, confess to yourself whether you would have to die if writing were denied you. This before all: ask yourself in the quietest hour of your night: must I write? Dig down into yourself for a deep answer. And if this should be in the affirmative, if you may meet this solemn question with a strong and simple 'I must', then build your life according to this necessity; your life must, right to its most unimportant and insignificant hour, become a token and a witness of this impulse. Then draw near to Nature. Then try, as if you were one of the first men, to say what you see and experience and love and lose. Do not write love poems; avoid at first those forms which are too familiar and usual: they are the most difficult, for great and fully matured strength is needed to make an individual contribution where good and in part brilliant traditions exist in plenty. Turn therefore from the

common themes to those which your own everyday life affords; depict your sorrows and desires, your passing thoughts and belief in some kind of beauty—depict all that with heartfelt, quiet, humble sincerity and use to express yourself the things that surround you, the images of your dreams and the objects of your memory. If your everyday life seems poor to you, do not accuse it; accuse yourself, tell yourself you are not poet enough to summon up its riches; since for the creator there is no poverty and no poor or unimportant place. And even if you were in a prison whose walls allowed none of the sounds of the world to reach your senses—would you not still have always your childhood, that precious, royal richness, that treasure house of memories? Turn your attention there. Try to raise the submerged sensations of that distant past; your personality will grow stronger, your solitude will extend itself and will become a twilit dwelling which the noise of others passes by in the distance.—And if from this turning inwards, from this sinking into your private world, there come verses, you will not think to ask anyone whether they are good verses. You will not attempt, either, to interest journals in these works: for you will see in them you own dear genuine possession, a portion and a voice of your life. A work of art is good if it has grown out of necessity. In this manner of its origin lies its true estimate: there is no other. Therefore, my dear Sir, I could give you no advice but this: to go into yourself and to explore the depths whence your life wells forth; at its source you will find the answer to the question whether you must create. Accept it as it sounds, without enquiring too closely into every word. Perhaps it will turn out that you are called to be an artist. Then take your fate upon yourself and bear it, its burden and its greatness, without ever asking for that reward which might come from without. For the creator must be a world for himself, and find everything within himself, and in Nature to which he has attached himself.

Perhaps however, after this descent into yourself and into your aloneness, you will have to renounce your claim to become a poet; (it is sufficient, as I have said, to feel that one could live without writing, in order not to venture it at all). But even then this introversion which I beg of you has not been in vain. Your life will at all events find thenceforward its individual paths; and that they may be good and rich and far reaching I wish for you more than I can say.

What more shall I say to you? Everything seems to me to have its proper emphasis; I would finally just like to advise you to grow through your development quietly and seriously; you can interrupt it in no more violent manner than by looking outwards, and expecting answer from outside to questions which perhaps only your innermost feeling in your most silent hour can answer.

This passage is clear enough, but perhaps some additional points should be made. The poet is one who thinks in poetry, and who, very often, cannot understand easily except in poetry. I would say to the young poem-writer, 'Do you feel that there is any truth outside poetry?' If he answers, 'No', then he may be a poet, for his answer must mean that for him his awareness of truths of fact or philosophy or religion cannot be separated from his necessity to give that awareness its only real presence in poetry. I would ask the young poem-writer also 'Do you ever wish that you did not write poems?' If his answer is, 'No', then it is likely that he has not yet begun to face the emotional and spiritual agonies which are involved in facing steadily and courageously the most fundamental aspects of one's being. If he says, 'Yes', and says it with feeling, then maybe he has already realized that to write a true poem is to bring every human faculty into play, to bind these faculties together, as it were, into one faculty, and to employ it with every ounce of nervous energy he can command, to explore intuitions that may cause him to lose his sense of identity and his grip upon reason. Those that never find themselves in danger are those who never commit themselves wholly to their art.

In any teaching situation the vast majority of the students will prove to be poem-writers and not poets. The title *poet* is an honour to which only a few in any generation should aspire. It is not an honour given by public recognition, or by any kind of examination. A man who has published twenty books of poetry may be a poem-maker rather than a poet, and a man who has published little or nothing may be a poet for all that. The title is one for the individual writer to claim, in humility and awe, when he is convinced that he is not only writing poems but is absolutely committed, and inextricably involved in poetry, and that the poems he has made include a sufficient number which reach into the depths of his being for him to know that to be a poet is to be a servant and not a master. I was asked recently when I first considered myself to be a poet. I had to think for a long time. The conviction had been slow in coming. Finally, I said that the first time I called myself a poet and meant the title to be more than an approximation used loosely in conversation to refer to someone who made poems was when I had completed my third book. 'And then', I added, 'there were periods when I doubted. There are still periods when I doubt.' I could have added also that these times of doubt, when the poems do not come or prove to be merely competent, are times of sickness. I feel physically unwell; I have no joy in life; I am only partly alive. I survive these periods by attempting to serve poetry in other ways—by writing about it, by teaching young poem-writers, and by making collages in which I can remain creative and imaginative until the words return. Every poet needs some other creative activity, one in which he can utilize his psychic energy and his imagination, if he is to avoid breakdown. Many poets paint. Some play musical instruments. Many turn to crafts and become obsessed with gardening or carpentry. One fine poet, John Knight, is a maker of most superb wines. This may all seem trivial, but a poet cannot exist without making; he cannot live if he does not feed himself with symbols; he cannot go on living if he is not to go on exploring and discovering. The poet does not, like many authors, write in order to live. He lives in order to write. If he cannot write, then his reason for living is gone.

It is this, of course, which accounts for much of the suffering experienced by poets and artists of all kinds. No one can write continually. There must be dry patches. At these times the poet faces meaningless nothingness. He may turn, as many have turned, to an orthodox or unorthodox faith, to the Church or to the bottle. He may, in an effort to give his life some other reason for continuing, take a mistress or another job. He may persuade himself to fall in love, or enter a monastery, or climb a mountain. If he does not do something he knows he may sink so deep into the Slough of Despond that he will never extricate himself. It must therefore be said quite unequivocally that the life of a poet is one which brings suffering, and, moreover, frequently brings suffering upon the poet's friends and family as well as upon himself.

There is, of course, no easy solution to this kind of problem. The wise poet is one who contrives to get through his periods of despair without doing anything that may harm any poems that just conceivably may be given him in the future. He does not become an alcoholic; he does not get kicks from drugs; he does not do anything that may damage the quickness of his mind or the delicacy of his nervous system. Poets, however, are not always wise, and, in these periods of sterility it is common for poets to become so convinced that they will never write again that they begin what amounts to a slow suicide by one means or another. The list of poets who have suffered nervous or mental breakdowns, of differing degrees of seriousness, is large. In our own century we can point to Robert Lowell, Ann Sexton, Sylvia Plath, David Gascoyne, Randal Jarrell, Theodore Roethke, all of whom have themselves referred to such crises in their work or whose trials have become matters of public record. These breakdowns are not necessarily ones resulting from the despair attendant upon temporary (one prays) sterility. Some result quite simply from the strains and stresses of the job.

This is the dark side of the picture. It is one that must be shown, however, for the struggles and tribulations are inextricably involved in

145

the achievements and the joy. That joy can be, at its most intense, sometimes terrible, in that the strength of the poem as it thrusts its way into existence can frighten one. There is a poem by Kathleen Raine which is an invocation to the spirit of poetry to permit the poem to be born, which is both a cry of agony and, because it is itself the poem it desires, a cry of triumph.

Invocation

There is a poem on the way,
there is a poem all round me,
the poem is in the near future,
the poem is in the upper air
above the foggy atmosphere
it hovers, a spirit
that I would make incarnate.
Let my body sweat
let snakes torment my breast
my eyes be blind, ears deaf, hands distraught
mouth parched, uterus cut out,
belly slashed, back lashed,
tongue slivered into thongs of leather
rain stones inserted in my breasts,
head severed,

if only the lips may speak,
if only the god will come.

When the poem of real intensity does come, the poet loses all sense of his own identity. He is merely the gateway and obstruction through which the poem must move. At such times he may well feel in a state of near-trance, almost in a state of suspended animation. He is, at that point in time, alive only to produce the poem, and in all other ways dead. I found myself expressing something of this in a poem recently:

Endure. Endure.
I make no words.
Words wake.

Rigor attends.
I stiffen.
The coffin speaks.

There was a
bird from my mouth.
I shudder slowly

back into breath
and sleep.

The poem extends.

The poet feels only fully awake when he is the vehicle for a poem. The rest of life may be pleasant, but it does not have that intense awareness which, having once experienced, he demands again and again. In poetry he feels that he sees through the veil of appearances into realities that extend beyond the confines of this life into territories of the spiritual and eternal. Even in his most mundane, most commonsensical poems, he feels a little of this. The reward of the poet is not financial, and is rarely public acclaim. It is the reward of feeling part of a spiritual universe vaster than that perceptible to the reason; it is the reward of feeling the soul growing in understanding and strength, though the mind may be puzzled and the body fail. If one can in any way help anyone to sense only a little of this in his own experience then one has done far more than help him to write poems. One has opened gateways to the mystery and majesty of eternal life.

Appendix

The Technology of Verse: A Guide

The information given here is intended more for reference than for close reading. Most young poets neither care, nor need to care, about such terms as epanorthosis and hypercatalexis. Very few indeed will ever feel impelled to compose a triolet or a pantoum and almost none are likely to hazard the intricacies of a canzone. Nevertheless, there are some who will find some of this information interesting and who will find it stimulating to experiment with intricate verse structures, and as the information given here is not, to my knowledge, to be found all together in any other book at present in print, there is, I feel, some justification for presenting it. I would, however, for the benefit of any young writer who grows too excited over these matters like to attach a statement similar to that upon cigarette packets in North America. *Warning: Over-indulgence in verse technique may be dangerous to your health.*

A Guide to Rhyme

Let us first of all make the point that rhyme, properly considered, occurs when two similar sounds are placed so as to echo one another. Rhyme does not have to be at the end of the line; nor does it have to be of the simple *mat–cat* variety. It can be varied in intensity, and in complexity. Let us look at full rhyme first of all.

FULL RHYMES

I. *Rime Riche.* This appears rarely in English, but was used extensively by the French poet, Victor Hugo. It consists of the repetition of a word which has two or more meanings in such a way that the first appearance carries one meaning and its second another. The Canadian poet Daryl Hine has experimented with this form of rhyme, as in the following poem:

A Present

Spring is late and I am going blind.
In his dark room my neighbour draws the blind
In order to develop. What? A film
Taken last summer. Underneath the chemical film
Of free association our features are still bright.
'Bruno wasn't really very bright,'
I write in my commonplace book, and pour myself a drink.
This winter is interminable. I drink
Too much. My neighbour doesn't drink at all.
But in his dark room he will work all
Night, developing the past.
I think of the future chronically, of the past
On occasion; never, never of the present.
Each day, cold and dimmer, is like a birthday present.

This illustrates *Rime Riche* at its purest. Another variety is shown by the opening lines of Austin Clarke's poem, *Marian Chimes.*

> Four times an hour the same peal
> Casts up our appeal
> And minutes that borrow a hood
> Cloister the neighbourhood
> And parish. Early to late,
> Rings our apostolate
> For Mary Immaculate . . .

This is not really *Rime Riche* at all, but it has a similar effect. In each case the first word of the rhyming series (we could call this word the *rhyme-agent*) is a complete word, and the following rhyming words (they are in fact the Rhymes proper) include this word as a final syllable.

II. *Masculine Rhyme.* This is a rhyme on one syllable, the rhymes repeating the final vowel-consonant combination of the rhyme-agent, e.g. cat/mat, bent/went, card/lard. This is only true masculine rhyme when an exact repetition of sound occurs, and not when the same letters result in a slightly different sound as in rhyming the proper name, Ned, with the last syllable of the word Delighted, or as in rhyming Cough with Bough. The former is a case of *weakened rhyme* and the latter a case of *eye-rhyme.*

III. *Feminine Rhyme.* This is a rhyme on two syllables, the rhymes repeating both the final and the penultimate vowel-consonant combinations of the rhyme-agent, e.g. tapping/rapping, coldly/boldly, leeward/seaward, effusion/delusion. When the rhymes repeat only a part of the *rhyme-agent's* penultimate syllable, as in Dilution/Oration this is not a case of *feminine rhyme* at all, but of *enriched masculine rhyme.* There are other common variants of *feminine rhyme* also. Frequently, while the final syllables of the *rhyme-agent* and the *rhyme* are identical the penultimate syllables are not, though there are enough common factors to give the illusion of a precise feminine rhyme. Thus we may get devotion/diversion, sabine/saline, riddle/ripple. These cases differ from those of *enriched masculine rhyme* by having an additional point of similarity between the rhyme-agent and the rhyme; they are not, however, true feminine rhymes. If we need a term for them it might be sensible to register that they have pretty well the same effect as feminine rhymes, however, and call them *crypto-feminine.*

IV. *Trisyllabic Rhyme.* This is, as its name indicates, a rhyme upon three syllables, e.g. indicate/vindicate, eluding/deluding, revision/division. The more syllables one uses in rhyming, the more variations are possible. Thus there is a near-trisyllabic rhyme which is more frequently used than the trisyllabic rhyme proper. Examples of this are supposing/reposing, regression/digression, involving/revolving. Here, the feminine rhyme has been enriched by the addition of a further consonantal parallel. A feminine rhyme would be session/profession; enriched, it could be changed to digression/regression, as above. We must call this variation *enriched feminine rhyme*. *Crypto-trisyllabic rhyme* takes place when we have such variations as hesitate/necessitate where the *s* and *ss* are pronounced differently but are, nevertheless, so close in sound as to make it ridiculous to call the instance an example of enriched feminine rhyme. Another example of crypto-trisyllabic rhyme is delectation/lactation, where the vowel sounds in the antepenultimate syllables differ, but are preceded by identical consonants.

We are now, however, dealing with mere ingenuities and rarities. In fact trisyllabic rhyme is rarely used in English except for comic effects, and rhymes of more than three syllables are so rarely used as to make labelling them unnecessary. All these full rhymes are difficult for the tyro to handle consistently. They have emphatic effects which disturb the flow of the verse, and, unless one is extremely deft, they cause one to distort the poem. The beginner would do better, having noted these kinds of rhyme, to turn to the next category.

NEAR RHYMES, OR HALF RHYMES

I. *Para-Rhyme.* This occurs when the rhyming agent and the rhymes have different vowel sounds but identical final and penultimate consonantal groupings. This kind of rhyme was first labelled and used consistently by Wilfred Owen. Examples are: greet/grate, bland/blind, ride/road.

II. *Feminine Para-Rhyme.* There are two forms of this, one in which both vowel sounds differ and one in which only one does. The three final consonant groupings of the rhyme-agent and the rhymes are identical in both cases. Examples of the first kind are devote/divert, palace/police. It is, however, the second kind which is more frequently observed, e.g. falter/filter, relate/relight, attune/attain, punning/pinning.

III. *Weakened Rhyme.* This is a rhyme in which the rhyming syllable is accented in one word and unaccented (or weak) in the other. A weakened masculine rhyme would be Ned/delighted, as already mentioned, and also Pant/participant. The vowel sounds differ, of course, because one is stressed and the other not, but they are still closely enough related for us not to use the term *consonance*.

IV. *Unstressed Rhyme.* Here the rhyming syllable is unaccented in all

6+

cases, e.g. Wonder/liver, riding/singing, river/under. This almost frequently appears as a variation of enriched masculine rhyme as in lover/ever, harried/buried, potion/mission. If the rhyming syllables end with consonants that are sounded the effect is more emphatic than if they do not. There is a considerable difference between rhyming wonder/liver and rhyming London/liven.

V. *Trailing Rhyme.* Here one word trails an unstressed syllable after its rhyming one, while the other does not, e.g. shove/lover, light/brighter, cold/boldly, pit/written. This is less a kind of rhyme than a fashion of placing rhyme, however.

VI. *Consonance.* This is not usually regarded as a kind of rhyme, though it is difficult to see why not. Here the linked words simply have their final consonantal groupings in common, e.g., end/blind, put/bet, will/hall. Alliteration is a form of consonance, and the term is generally used to describe words which have their initial consonants in common. It is confusing when it is used to describe other phenomena. *The Dirty dog died* is a case of alliteration, in my view, and *The dog hid under the door* is a case of consonance. Consonance is used internally to a greater degree than all other more complicated types of rhyme and many poems are given their pattern quality by consonantal clusters.

VII. *Assonance,* is not usually regarded as a kind of rhyme, either. It occurs when the words have vowel sounds in common, e.g. sane/late, door/caught, part/guard. Assonance is not as easy to use effectively as consonance, for the vowel sounds are often qualified by the effect of adjacent consonants. Thus the first *a* sound in *far away* is so altered by the sounding of the *r* that it differs from the *a* sound in *farm*. Internal assonance on all but the most emphatic vowel sounds tends to be less effective than consonance. On the other hand, assonance can take on the force of full rhyme when the vowel sound comes at the end of the line as in sea/me, try/fly, no/go, which would all be regarded as *masculine rhymes* by any reasonable reader. Even slightly less emphatic cases of end-consonance, however, seem close to masculine rhymes, e.g., purely/tidy. Of course purely/lovely *would* be a masculine rhyme, as would slow/grow, or lover/liver, though the latter, as we have pointed out, would be *unstressed masculine rhyme.*

All these labels matter very little in themselves. They are useful when one is attempting to analyse a poem's structure, but their main value is the way in which they enable us to see clearly the many varieties of rhyming devices. The beginner, writing proportional verse, and attempting to write stress verse, will find that attempting also to use the less rigid forms of rhyme will, to some extent, educate his ear. You cannot make a rhyme work unless its chime occurs exactly in the right spot. Consequently, practice in rhyming leads to a feeling for the proportions of verse and for rhythm and metre. It also leads one to appreciate that a poem must have certain high-points of verbal drama, and that these must be arranged for maximum effect.

A Guide to Metrical Feet

English metre is conventionally divided up into feet. These are based largely upon classical metres and only a small number of them really occur with any regularity in English. A full list runs as follows:

FEET OF TWO SYLLABLES

Iamb	x/	before, alone, despair
Trochee	/x	gently, venture, over
Spondee	//	Dodo, hatrack, flywheel
Pyrrhic	xx	in the, at a, of a

FEET OF THREE SYLLABLES

Amphibrach	x/x	Denoted, remotely, attending, division
Amphimacer or Cretic	/x/	Outermost, Peregrine, Dragoman
Anapaest	xx/	the canoe, to betray
Dactyl	/xx	hurriedly, bargaining, wanderer
Molossus	///	big bad wolf, ding dong bell
Tribrach	xxx	into the, and as if
Bacchic	//x	rolled over, old woman
Anti-Bacchic	x//	an old man, a lone wolf

FEET OF FOUR SYLLABLES

Antispast	x//x	the vast darkness, a strange vision
Choriamb	/xx/	cold and alone, clearly aware
Di-iamb	x/x/	alone again, before the mast
Di-trochee	/x/x	lonely darkness, future trouble
Epitrite	x///	a big bad wolf
	/x//	hit a bad wolf
	//x/	bad wolf destroyed
	///x	bad wolf ended
Ionic a majore	//xx	lone wanderer

Ionic a minore	xx//	the betrayed girl
Paeon	/xxx	Dimly in a, Singing of a,
	x/xx	a wanderer
	xx/x	in the morning
	xxx/	into the dark
Proceleusmatic	xxxx	at an undis-, in and of the,

It is obvious from this list that most of these terms are unnecessary. The feet of four syllables can, after all, be equally well described as being cases of disyllabic feet being combined. There is no excuse for the di-iamb or di-trochee, certainly. Alternating iambic and trochaic feet turn up often enough for there to be some reason for retaining the terms Antispast and Choriamb, however.

The trouble with these terms is that one can often describe a given line a number of different ways. Take, for example, the perfectly reasonable rhythmic sequence:

$$x//x \ xx/x//.$$

Is this

iamb, trochee, pyrrhic, anti-bacchic

or

antispast, anapaest, anti-bacchic

or

iamb, dactyl, amphibrach, spondee?

The answer to the question lies in common sense. If a line can be judged to include one type of foot more than once, then one should base one's scansion upon that foot. Thus I would call our line catalectic antispastic trimeter with anapaestic substitution in the second foot.

The situation is complicated, however, by there being other terms to bother us. A line may consist of any number of feet, from one to seven. The terms are monometer, dimeter, trimeter, tetrameter, pentameter, hexameter (or alexandrine), and heptameter. A line of iambic heptameter is called a fourteener, because it has fourteen syllables.

There are, also, a number of terms for mixed meters and for rarities. An eight-foot dactyllic line is called an octometer. An eleven-syllable line is called a hendecasyllable. When these, or any lines, are perfectly regular and precisely of the right length they are termed acatalectic; if they are short by a syllable or half-foot they are termed catalectic, and if short by a whole foot brachycatalectic. If they are a half-foot or a whole foot too long they are termed hypercatalectic. Anacrusis occurs when one or more unstressed syllables are added to the beginning of a line.

Perhaps the most useful of all these special terms, however, are the following:

Substitution: which refers to one foot being substituted for another.

Epanaphora: which refers to the repetition of the same word or words at the beginning of successive lines.

Epanorthosis: which refers to the repetition of word or words at other points than the beginnings of the lines.

Enjambement, or rove-over: which refers to the way in which a sentence or phrase may run over, without pause, from one line to the next.

End-stopped: refers, of course, to lines where the sense is coterminous with the line itself, and the lines are therefore self-contained in meaning.

With this armoury of terms available it becomes really quite difficult to approach verse making with a clear head. Nevertheless, they do enable us to see, through all the trees, the timber of a truth. Metre, properly described, consists in the repetition of rhythmic units in a recognizable pattern. We may add to this that almost all persuasive speech is rhythmical. Many political speeches are, in our loose sense of the term, metrical, even though there is no label for their recurrent rhythmical patterns. And a good deal of so-called *free verse* can, in fact, be described as metre because it possesses a recognizable rhythmic pattern.

A Guide to Stanza Forms

There are many established stanza forms in English, and new ones are being invented every year, though very few of these turn out to be of more than limited utility. Each established stanza form has its own limitations and advantages and provides a different way of looking. It is therefore worth while examining the main ones for the sake of those who find themselves stimulated by technical problems, and also because no book on the practice of poetry could be regarded as adequate if it did not provide this information.

I. STANZAS OF TWO LINES

These are called couplets, when rhymed, or distiches when not. Their usage differs from that of continuous couplets only in that, properly speaking, the sense of the distich should be complete; there should be no rove-over from one stanza to the next.

II. THREE-LINE STANZAS, OR TERCETS

a. *Triplets*. These rhyme aaa, bbb, ccc, and so on. Tennyson used the form in *Two Voices*, and Cowper in *My Mary*.

b. *Terza rima*. This consists of a series of tercets, each stanza linked to the following one by rhyme, thus aba, bcb, cdc. A poem in terza rima usually concludes with one separate line or with a quatrain, thus efe, fgf, g, or efe, fgfg, though some end efe, ff, or efe, fee, or even efe fgg. The most famous *terza rima* is that used by Dante in *La Divine Commedia*. In Italian the rhymes are feminine. British poets tend to use masculine rhyme, or even near-rhyme, as does Archibald Macleish in *Conquistador*. Some vary the rigour of the form by making the metre irregular, as did Auden in *The Sea and the Mirror*. Thomas Kinsella's *Downstream* is a more recent example.

c. *Tercet with a short last line*. This may rhyme aaa, bbb, and so on, or aab, ccb, ddb, or aab, ccb, dde, ffe; in this last case the tercets are obviously grouped into pairs by the rhyme-scheme and therefore really appear to be a form of six-line stanza with a strong median pause. George Herbert uses this form in *Life and the Flowers*.

d. *Other variations.* These include tercets with lines of different lengths. The triplet can easily cope with quite excessive metrical irregularities because of the emphatic nature of the rhyme-pattern.

Thus, we might, frivolously, write

> Our ginger cat
> will never sleep on his mat;
> he prefers my hat.

Or

> Though he never sleeps on his mat
> our cat
> simply loves my hat

One need not, however, be frivolous:

> Along the track
> the hedges hung thick and black,
> and the leaves like rags were drab and wet and slack.

Thomas Hardy used unequal lines in tercets and triplets in many poems.

III. FOUR-LINE STANZAS OR QUATRAINS

a. *Common measure.* This consists of a quatrain alternating iambic tetrameter with iambic trimeter and rhyming abab. It is also known as the hymnal stanza, as it is so frequently found in hymnals.

b. *Hymnal long measure.* This consists of a quatrain of iambic tetrameter rhyming either abab, or abcb.

d. *Hymnal short measure.* This consists of a quatrain composed of two iambic trimeter lines, followed by a tetrameter, and a trimeter, rhyming either abab or abcb.

e. *Ballad stanza.* Though there is no rule as to metre, many ballads are written in common measure, only rhyming abcb instead of abab.

f. *In Memoriam, or envelope stanza.* This consists of four iambic tetrameter lines, rhyming abba. It was used to most effect by Tennyson in *In Memoriam*.

g. *Other varieties.* These are obviously only numberable by indulging in some calculation of all possible permutations and combinations. Some, however, occur often enough to be worth noting.

One is the stanza used by Lewis Carroll in *Jabberwocky*. It is a quatrain rhyming abab, the first three lines being iambic tetrameter and the last iambic trimeter.

Another well-known quatrain is that used by Fitzgerald for his version of the *Rubaiyat of Omar Khayyam*. It consists of four iambic pentameter lines rhyming aaba. Swinburne uses a variety of this form in his *Laus Veneris*, but linked the stanzas in pairs by rhyming their b lines.

Another stanza form is the *Sapphic*, so called because it is modelled on the verse of Sappho. The first three lines are of five feet, these being, in order, a trochee, a spondee, a dactyl, a trochee and a spondee. In English practice the first and third feet are sometimes a dactyl and a trochee rather than the other way round, and the final foot is not infrequently a trochee. The fourth line of the stanza is made up of a dactyl followed by a spondee, though here again, English writers have often replaced the spondee with a trochee. There is an example of English Sapphics on page 40 of this book.

Other variations can be found in Browning's *A Woman's Last Word*, and *A Pretty Woman*, Byron's *On this Day I Complete My Thirty Sixth Year*, and Longfellow's *Endymion*.

IV. FIVE-LINE STANZAS OR QUINTAINS

There are no established forms for the quintain. It has been used effectively by many poets and in many ways. The most usual rhyme scheme is ababa, or abaca. Variation of line length is frequent. Sometimes the two central lines are only half the normal line length; this makes the quintain appear to be a reorganized quatrain. One of the most interesting quintains is that used by Edmund Waller in his finest poem:

> Go, lovely Rose!
> Tell her that wastes her time and me
> That now she knows,
> When I resemble her to thee,
> How sweet and fair she seems to be.

The last line of the quintain often appears to be an elaboration of, or appendage to, a thought which is contained within the quatrain. Shelley uses the form in his *Ode to a Skylark*, thus:

> Hail to thee, Blithe Spirit.
> Bird thou never wert,
> that in heaven or near it
> pourest thy full heart
> in profuse strains of unpremeditated art

In some stanzas of this poem, and of others using a quintain with a long fifth line, the last line has so obvious a central pause that the whole appears to be a reorganized sestet.

A more cohesive form of the quintain using different lengths of line is that used by George Herbert in *The Steadfast Life*. The first and fourth lines are the short ones, and the stanza rhymes abbab.

V. SIX-LINE STANZAS OR SESTETS

Again, there are many varieties. The most frequent regular form rhymes abcbdb; this is also used with the rhyming lines rather shorter than the others, as by Longfellow in *A Slave's Dream*. Sometimes the form looks like a quatrain with a following couplet or distich that sums up all that has occurred previously, or elaborates upon it. This is occasionally true of The Burns stanza, which rhymes aaabab, the b lines being diameter, the remainder being tetrameter.

Examples of good sestets can be found in Herrick's *To Blossoms*, and Shelley's *Death*. A useful form is the regular stanza rhyming abcabc, for the rhymes are far enough apart to be unobtrusive.

VI. SEVEN-LINE STANZAS

a. *Rhyme royal or the Troilus stanza.* This form was first used in English by Chaucer for his *Troilus and Criseyde*. It consists of seven decasyllabic lines rhyming ababbcc. The metre is usually iambic.

b. *Other varieties.* These include stanzas rhyming ababccc, abcbabc, and abcbdbb. In a stanza of this length it is possible to so separate the rhyming lines as to make the rhymes unobtrusive and thus give the poem greater fluidity, as in the stanza rhyming abcabca.

VII. EIGHT-LINE STANZAS

Ottava rima is the most famous of these. It consists of eight lines of iambic pentameter rhyming abababcc. It is used most successfully by Byron in *Don Juan* and by W. H. Auden in his *Letter to Lord Byron*.

Another form used by Chaucer is rhymed ababbcbc. It was taken from the French.

Many eight-line stanzas are really combinations of established quatrain forms, as is the stanza used by Lovelace in *To Althea from Prison*, which rhymes ababcdcd. Sir Walter Scott, in his *Helvellyn*, used a long line of four amphibrachs, the second, fourth, and eighth lines being catalectic, rhyming it ababaaab.

> I climb'd the dark brow of the mighty Hellvellyn,
>> Lakes and mountains beneath me gleam'd misty and wide;
> All was still, save by fits, when the eagle was yelling,
>> And starting around me the echoes replied.
> On the right, Striden-edge round the Red-tarn was bending,
> And Catchedicam its left verge was defending,
> One huge nameless rock in the front was ascending,
>> When I mark'd the sad spot where the wanderer had died.

It is possible to find many varieties of eight-line stanzas and comparatively easy to find little-used combinations.

VIII. NINE-LINE STANZA

a. *The Spenserian stanza.* This is the most notable of all nine-line stanzas. It consists of eight pentameter lines followed by an alexandrine, rhyming ababbcbcc. It was invented by Spenser and used by him in *The Faerie Queene*. It is also used by Byron in *Childe Harold*, by James Thomson in *The Castle of Indolence*, and by Burns in *The Cotter's Saturday Night*.

IX. STANZAS OF TEN, ELEVEN AND TWELVE LINES

These are subject to so many variations that it is hardly worth while to discuss them. It is worth looking, however, at their use by Gray in *On a Distant Prospect of Eton College*, by Browning in *The Last Ride Together*, and in *Too Late*, and by Tennyson in *Mariana*. Most of these long stanzas can be regarded as being made up of a combination of other stanza forms, these shorter forms being linked together by the exigencies of syntax more often than by common rhymes.

The really golden era of British metrics was the nineteenth century. Though there were many metrical innovations made during the Renaissance and some poets, such as Campion, were enormously dextrous, blank verse and the heroic couplet dominated most non-lyric poetry during the period 1620 to 1820, and it was only when the second generation of Romantics began to study both classical and native metres and forms that British poetry became as inventive as the list above suggests.

If one were to list the most interesting metrists in English one would not, necessarily, come up with the names of the greatest poets. Such a list would, however, certainly include Shelley, Byron, Tennyson, Browning, and Swinburne as well as Thomas Hardy and W. H. Auden. Others whose works deserve special attention in this regard are W. S. Graham (for his use of the three-beat line), John Betjeman (for his use of neat stanzaic forms), and Ogden Nash (for his extraordinary control of unequal rhyming lines, however facetious they may be). Dylan Thomas's mastery of complex stanza forms is shown in *Fern Hill, Poem in October,* and *Vision and Prayer*.

Thomas did not, however, make use of any of the *Twenty-Four Official Metres* of his native Wales. These are described in detail in Gwyn Williams' *An Introduction to Welsh Poetry* (Faber, 1953), but they have rarely been used by poets writing in English. That they can, however, be used has been proved by Rolfe Humphries who has written poetry in all of them. Anyone concerned to explore these forms should read Humphries' *Green Armor on Green Ground* (Scribners, 1956).

Nevertheless, in the twentieth century only a small number of poets have chosen to work in complex stanzas and metres and abstract forms. Thus we tend to associate these modes of writing with a nineteenth-century sensibility alien to ours, and suspect they necessarily involve either romantic posturing or mere ingenuity.

And yet, if one looks at the finest modern poems, however *free* they appear to be at first, one soon discovers that they can easily be related to previously fashionable strict forms and strict metres. William Carlos Williams' *To Asphodel that Greeny Flower* (his finest poem), Pound's *Homage to Sextus Propertius*, many of Charles Olsen's best poems, and certainly all of Wallace Stevens', have, behind them, a solidity of structure and a disciplined use of rhythm and line-length that relates them not to the simple but to some of the most complex verse forms and metres of the past.

A Guide to Obsessive Forms[1]

The three main obsessive forms are the *villanelle,* the *sestina,* and the *canzone.* Of these the villanelle is much the most interesting and useful to examine, for it has received a good deal of attention in our own century and there have been some interesting variations upon it.

The villanelle is a poem of nineteen lines. These are divided into five three-line stanzas and one concluding stanza of four lines. There are only two rhymes in the whole, and the first line of the poem is also the last line of the second and fourth stanzas and the penultimate line of the poem. The third line of the poem is also the third line of the third and fifth stanzas and the last line of the poem. The form originated with the troubadours of Provence and was imported into England in Chaucer's time. It received little use thereafter until the late nineteenth century when, like the ballade, triolet, rondeau, and rondel, it became popular with writers of light verse, as well as with a small number of serious poets.

Oscar Wilde retained the original pastoral tone, and used the refrain as apostrophe and interrogation.

Theocritus

O singer of Persephone!
  In the dim meadows desolate
Dost thou remember Sicily?

Still through the ivy flits the bee
  Where Amaryllis lies in state;
O Singer of Persephone!

Simaetha calls on Hecate
  And hears the wild dogs at the gate;
Dost thou remember Sicily?

---

[1] i.e. forms of which the characteristic feature is the frequent repetition of particular verbal elements.

> Still by the light and laughing sea
>   Poor Polypheme bemoans his fate;
> O Singer of Persephone!
>
> And still in boyish rivalry
>   Young Daphnis challenges his mate;
> Dost thou remember Sicily?
>
> Slim Lacon keeps a goat for thee,
>   For thee the jocund shepherds wait;
> O Singer of Persephone!
> Dost thou remember Sicily?

Austin Dobson, in an affectionate, slight, poem perceived that the refrain must have some dramatic justification, and not be merely a rhetorical decoration. Thus he used the repetition to create a feeling of obsession about the passing of time.

When I Saw You Last, Rose

> When I saw you last, Rose,
>   You were only so high;—
> How fast the time goes!
>
> Like a bud ere it blows,
>   You just peeped at the sky,
> When I saw you last, Rose!
>
> Now your petals unclose,
>   Now your May-time is nigh;—
> How fast the time goes!
>
> And a life,—how it grows!
>   You were scarcely so shy,
> When I saw you last, Rose.
>
> In your bosom it shows
>   There's a guest on the sly;
> How fast the time goes!
>
> Is it Cupid? Who knows!
>   Yet you used not to sigh,
> When I saw you last, Rose;
> How fast the time goes!

When Edwin Arlington Robinson handled the form he chose to make both refrain lines expressive of an obsession, and he chose a situation to

which the recurrence of one thought expressed in the same simple words
would be appropriate.

The House On The Hill

They are all gone away,
    The House is shut and still,
There is nothing more to say.

Through broken walls and gray
    The winds blow bleak and shrill:
They are all gone away.

Nor is there one to-day
    To speak them good or ill:
There is nothing more to say.

Why is it then we stray
    Around the sunken sill?
They are all gone away,

And our poor fancy-play
    For them is wasted skill:
There is nothing more to say.

There is ruin and decay
    In the House on the Hill:
They are all gone away,
There is nothing more to say.

It was William Empson, however, in the 1930s who first perceived that
the villanelle could also include intellectual argument, and need not be
written in short tripping lines.

Missing Dates

Slowly the poison the whole blood stream fills.
It is not the effort nor the failure tires.
The waste remains, the waste remains and kills.

It is not your system or clear sight that mills
Down small to the consequence a life requires;
Slowly the poison the whole blood stream fills.

They bled an old dog dry yet the exchange rills
Of young dog blood gave but a month's desires
The waste remains, the waste remains and kills.

It is the Chinese tombs and the slag hills
Usurp the soil, and not the soil retires.
Slowly the poison the whole blood stream fills.

Not to have fire is to be a skin that shrills.
The complete fire is death. From partial fires
The waste remains, the waste remains and kills.

It is the poems you have lost, the ills
From missing dates, at which the heart expires.
Slowly the poison the whole blood stream fills.
The waste remains, the waste remains and kills.

Empson's villanelles gave rise to villanelles by many younger poets in the 1950s. Most of these owed something to Empson's style, and were both ironic and despairing. Gordon Wharton's *Paradise Lost* is a good example of the fashionable content of the Villanelle in the 1950s.

Paradise Lost

The bean-feast's over, let's call it a day.
No more great jokes, Bright-eyes is looking grim;
The knives and forks are washed and put away.

No use complaining that we cannot stay,
We'll have to hitch our belts up and stay slim.
The bean-feast's over, let's call it a day.

No christian names come bounding out to play,
They line up by the door, are telling him
The knives and forks are washed and put away.

If he looks angry, well, he cannot say
He wasn't warned. I saw him dialling TIM—
The bean-feast's over, let's call it a day.

Bright-eyes is darling just once in a way,
But finds it difficult to keep in trim.
The knives and forks are washed and put away.

I hope it thunders for the skies are grey.
Before we go ought we to sing a hymn?
The bean-feast's over, let's call it a day,
The knives and forks are washed and put away.

The famous villanelle of Dylan Thomas, was written earlier. He chose to use the refrain for apostrophe.

Do not go gentle into that good night

Do not go gentle into that good night,
Old age should burn and rave at close of day;
Rage, rage against the dying of the light.

Though wise men at their end know dark is right,
Because their words have forked no lightning they
Do not go gentle into that good night.

Good men, the last wave by, crying how bright
Their frail deeds might have danced in a green bay,
Rage, rage against the dying of the light.

Wild men who caught and sang the sun in flight,
And learn, too late, they grieved it on its way,
Do not go gentle into that good night.

Grave men, near death, who see with blinding sight
Blind eyes could blaze like meteors and be gay,
Rage, rage against the dying of the light.

And you, my father, there on the sad height,
Curse, bless, me now with your fierce tears, I pray.
Do not go gentle into that good night.
Rage, rage against the dying of the light.

Many poets in the fifties and sixties used *terza rima* in poems of villanelle
length, and several also twisted the villanelle form. There are a number of
ways in which this can be done. One is to get all the advantages of
obsessive recurrence, and lose the disadvantage of there being little room
to say anything of importance before a refrain line comes round again,
by weaving *terza rima* stanzas into the villanelle, thus making it twice as
long and more discursive. The *terza rima* stanzas, should, however, be
linked by rhyme to the villanelle stanzas, if the poem is not going to
lose unity. Here is an experiment of my own following this pattern.

Colours

In colours all the wisdom man may prize
within this fallen world are shown, for know
colours are creatures of the fallen eyes.

At the beginning of days the white world lies
quiet and cold as early may or snows
new from eternal space; then colours rise,

a gradual glory on our troubled eyes.
After the innocence, light breaks to show
in colours all the wisdom man may prize,

A yellow sun flares on this land below
whose gold we praise, whose crowns are crowns of
    straw,
whose cats have golden eyes, and all we know

of good is gilded with that sun's disguise,
colouring each rule, each passing show;
colours are creatures of the fallen eyes,

incarnadine the endings of all days,
when blood's upon the countries of the skies,
and red lips are the total of love's praise

and in the evening yearn; heart's splendid lies
grow shadowy as night nears, for lovers know
in colours all the wisdom man may prize,

and blue, upon the palace as the plough,
foretells the coming dark that will allow
no brilliance to delight, for colours go

into the final dark, grey shadows rise
within each garden where tall lilies blow;
colours are creatures of the fallen eyes,

and in the night we lose their world to know
the darkness mercy spared our exile show
by absence all the white light that we grow

continually towards, whose loving eyes,
our day's beginning and life's ending, show
in colours all the wisdom man may prize;
colours are creatures of the fallen eyes.

Another method is to make the stanzas longer by a line and still use
two refrain lines. A section from Tony Connor's *The Seven Last Poems from
the Memoirs of Uncle Harry* illustrates the effectiveness of this method.

Invoke my grief's compendium:
it will be company on the way to Hell Gate;
the laughs we had are lying doggo,
and all the bottles are empty in the grate.

I had a myth as wise as your arsehole,
I sent that myth to work for the good of the state,
take it, wrapped in an ample pension,
to keep you company on the way to Hell Gate.

Where are the hopes we tossed between us?
Where are the dreams, the gay dreams of night?
A wind from the north's in my hollow molar,
and all the bottles are empty in the grate.

I had a heart as big as this planet:
What use in a small life is an organ so great?
I made a bomb and blew it to fragments,
they will be company on the way to Hell Gate.

When will the seed we sowed be flower?
When will my twisted walking stick take root?
My feet are frothed with encroaching ocean,
and all the bottles are empty in the grate.

I had a girl with alarm clock nipples
she came on time, but oh I rose too late;
put this useless thing in your pocket,
it will be company on the way to Hell Gate.

Aye: youth was rain on a lonely corner,
age: fifteen medals on a ragged coat;
now I've a room without a window,
and all the bottles are empty in the grate.

Tonight's a snake without a ladder,
and all the bottles are empty in the grate;
you can cheat yourself in the vacant places,
it will be company on the way to Hell Gate.

Another way is to retain two of the villanelle elements, the repetitions, and the three-line stanza, but organize them in another fashion. Kingsley Amis does this in a poem he called *The Voice of Authority: A Language Game.* He has here used the same end-words in the same order in each stanza, and ended each stanza with the same group of words.

Do this. Don't move. O'Grady says do this,
You get a move on, see, do what I say.
Look lively when I say O'Grady says.

Say this. Shut up. O'Grady says say this,
You talk fast without thinking what to say.
What goes is what I say O'Grady says.

Or rather let me put the point like this:
O'Grady says what goes is what I say
O'Grady says; that's what O'Grady says.

By substituting you can shorten this,
Since any god you like will do to say
The things you like, that's what O'Grady says.

The harm lies not in that, but in that this
Progression's first and last terms are I say
O'Grady says, not just O'Grady says.

Yet it's O'Grady must be out of this
Before what we say goes, not what we say
O'Grady says. Or so O'Grady says.

This poem of Amis's reminds one of the more elaborate forms of the
sestina and the canzone, in which the formula involves the repetition of
the same end-words in each stanza. This is, obviously, another obsessive
form. One example of a modern sestina may suffice: here is W. H.
Auden's *Have A Good Time*.

'We have brought you,' they said, 'a map of the country;
Here is the line that runs to the vats,
This patch of green on the left is the wood,
We've pencilled an arrow to point out the bay.
No thank you, no tea; why look at the clock.
Keep it? Of course. It goes with our love.

We shall watch your future and send our love.
We lived for years, you know, in the country.
Remember at week-ends to wind up the clock.
We've wired to our manager at the vats.
The tides are perfectly safe in the bay,
But whatever you do don't go to the wood.

There's a flying trickster in that wood,
And we shan't be there to help with our love.
Keep fit by bathing in the bay,
You'll never catch fever then in the country.
You're sure of a settled job at the vats
If you keep their hours and live by the clock.'

He arrived at last; it was time by the clock.
He crossed himself as he passed the wood;
Black against evening sky the vats
Brought tears to his eyes as he thought of their love;
Looking out over the darkening country,
He saw the pier in the little bay.

At the week-ends the divers in the bay
Distracted his eyes from the bandstand clock;
When down with fever and in the country
A skein of swans above the wood
Caused him no terror; he came to love
The moss that grew on the derelict vats.

And he has met sketching at the vats
Guests from the new hotel in the bay;
Now, curious, following his love,
His pulses differing from the clock,
Finds consummation in the wood
And sees for the first time the country.

Sees water in the wood and trees by the bay,
Hears a clock striking near the vats;
'This is your country and the home of love'.

The canzone is more complicated, and usually turns out to be dull. The degree of obsessiveness is strong, but the form is so lengthy that some amount of sheer argument is needed, and the argument must be in a limited number of terms, though the rules do allow the words to change a little as the poem develops. Here is my own experiment with this form.

Canzone

In every infancy the world of love
is swathed in sunlight, binding the vague hands
from any cold, from any other love
whose frozen light might eat into that love
life's acid terror, in hours' round control,
another larger womb held by her love
from prematurity, the flesh of love,
surpassed, come to its own, enfolding time
and space until the stir and lunge of time
claims love's release, and, making its own love,
stumbles towards new limits, as a child
unsteadily, and separate as a child.

The gradual entrance of the separate child
upon his love's inheritance makes love
both secret toy and councillor whom the child
emperor may run to as a child
for that dependence which has potent hands
to reinstate the emperor in the child
and make all terror seem a wayward child
of his own making that he can control
by a superior bearing, that control
his path towards the limits of the child,
an exploration that in course of time
will map a country he must lose to time.

Youth will not bow the knee to love or time
when he has finally put off the child
and left his little empire in good time
to conquer different continents, where time,
his sometime wayward servant, shows him love
to be made subject, saying that the time
has now come to advance, no more mark time
but enter citadels with eager hands
and plunder: soon he finds love on his hands
and he a subject conqueror; for a time
he calls his time a cheat, loses control,
and then retreats, is once more in control.

Love follows. One of them must gain control.
The juggling for position takes some time,
each bargaining from strength, each in control
of one half of the town, till his control
at last gives way completely; he, a child,
admits defeat yet sues for the control,
and she him conqueror under her control,
and both together weld the world of love,
and, for a time, all countries that they love
are theirs to rule, each land theirs to control
because they both are prisoners, in their hands
the fruits of bondage, glory in their hands.

But this new empire that with eager hands
they plunder and explore, map their control
over so many different nations, hands
them duties, shows them boundaries; their hands
should never be done plundering; those hands

now seem inept and clumsy as a child
that cannot grasp beyond the reach of child
until another birth brings stronger hands
and wider limits; world's love mapped, they love
beyond the flesh, cry for new worlds of love.

So to each lover in his world of love
life is new-born, and clumsy as a child
to grasp perception that will in its time
seem just another child seeking control
of world and world on world with tireless hands.

A Guide to Other Verse Forms

SONNET

The sonnet is a fourteen-line poem of iambic pentameters which is composed of two parts, the octet and the sestet. The division between the two may or may not be indicated by a space. The main forms of sonnet are the Shakespearean (rhyming ababcdcd efefgg), the Petrarchan (rhyming abbaabba cdecde), and the Miltonic (rhyming abbaabba cdcdcd). There are other variations upon the rhyming of the sestet. Among those that have been used are: cddcee, and cdccdc. Apart from Shakespeare and Milton the main English sonneteers include Sir Philip Sidney, Edmund Spenser (who produced a variation of his own), Elizabeth Barrett Browning, Dante Gabriel Rossetti, and Lord Alfred Douglas, who prided himself upon his precise use of the Petrarchan form.

TRIOLET

An eight-line poem rhyming abaaabab. The first, fourth, and seventh lines are identical; so are the second and the eighth.

> It's hard to write
> this kind of verse.
> It's made so tight
> it's hard to write;
> it makes you bite
> your nails and curse:
> it's hard to write
> this kind of verse.
>
> Robin Skelton

RONDEL

Originally a poem of two-, three-, four-, or five-line stanzas with only two rhymes, the Rondel was developed by Charles d'Orléans (1391–

176

1466) into a poem of thirteen lines in three stanzas, rhyming abba, abba, abbaa. The first two lines of the poem are also the last two lines of both the second and third stanzas.

The Wanderer

Love comes back to his vacant dwelling,—
   The old, old Love that we knew of yore!
   We see him stand by the open door,
With his great eyes sad, and his bosom swelling.

He makes as though in our arms repelling,
   He fain would lie as he lay before;—
Love comes back to his vacant dwelling,—
   The old, old Love that we knew of yore!

Ah! who shall help us from overspelling,
   That sweet forgotten, forbidden lore!
   E'en as we doubt in our hearts once more,
With a rush of tears to our eyelids welling,
Love comes back to his vacant dwelling.

                    Austin Dobson

RONDEAU

A poem of thirteen octosyllabic lines. The first half of the first line is repeated twice, once after the eighth line, and once after the thirteenth. The poem could thus be described as having thirteen lines with two additional half-lines. The rhyme scheme is aabbaabr, aabaar.

In Rotten Row

In Rotten Row a cigarette
I sat and smoked, with no regret
   For all the tumult that had been.
   The distances were still and green,

And streaked with shadows cool and wet
Two sweethearts on a bench were set,
Two birds among the boughs were met;
   So love and song were heard and seen
            In Rotten Row.

A horse or two there was to fret
The soundless sand; but work and debt,
   Fair flowers and falling leaves between,
   While clocks are chiming clear and keen,
A man may very well forget
        In Rotten Row.
         W. E. Henley

ROUNDEL

A poem of nine lines divided into three stanzas. The first phrase of the first line is repeated at the end of the first and last stanzas. The rhyme scheme is complex, as the refrain must also rhyme with other lines. If I bracket the refrain line, the scheme can be described as aba(b), bab, aba(b). A famous roundel is that by Swinburne.

The Roundel

A Roundel is wrought as a ring or a starbright sphere,
With craft of delight and with cunning of sound unsought,
That the heart of the hearer may smile if to pleasure his ear
        A roundel is wrought.

Its jewel of music is carven of all or of aught—
Love, laughter, or mourning–remembrance of rapture or fear—
That fancy may fashion to hang in the ear of thought.

As a bird's quick song runs round, and the hearts in us hear—
Pause answers to pause, and again the same strain caught,
So moves the device whence, round as a pearl or tear,
        A roundel is wrought.
        Algernon Charles Swinburne

BALLADE

A poem of twenty-eight lines, divided into three stanzas of eight lines and a final stanza of four. This last stanza, headed *Envoy* or *Envoi*, conventionally opens with the name of the person to whom the poem is supposedly sent or spoken, and sums up the tenor of the whole. The rhyme scheme is ababbcbc, ababbcbc, ababbcbc, bcbc. The last line is the same in all the stanzas.

A Ballade of Suicide

The gallows in my garden, people say,
Is new and neat and adequately tall.
I tie the noose on in a knowing way
As one that knots his necktie for a ball;
But just as all the neighbours—on the wall—
Are drawing a long breath to shout 'Hurray!'
The strangest whim has seized me. . . . After all
I think I will not hang myself to-day.

To-morrow is the time I get my pay—
My uncle's sword is hanging in the hall—
I see a little cloud all pink and grey—
Perhaps the Rector's mother will not call—
I fancy that I heard from Mr. Gall
That mushrooms could be cooked another way—
I never read the works of Juvenal—
I think I will not hang myself to-day.

The world will have another washing day;
The decadents decay; the pedants pall;
And H. G. Wells has found that children play,
And Bernard Shaw discovered that they squall;
Rationalists are growing rational—
And through thick woods one finds a stream astray,
So secret that the very sky seems small—
I think I will not hang myself to-day.

Envoi

Prince, I can hear the trumpet of Germinal,
The tumbrils toiling up the terrible way;
Even to-day your royal head may fall—
I think I will not hang myself to-day

G. K. Chesterton

There is also a 35-line version, the three stanzas each containing the ten
lines and the envoy five. The rhyme scheme for this form is ababbccdcd,
ababbccdcd, ababbccdcd, ccdcd. Swinburne used this form for his
version of Villon's *Ballade of the Hanged*.

A Ballade of François Villon

Bird of the bitter bright grey golden morn
   Scarce risen upon the dusk of dolorous years,
First of us all and sweetest singer born

Whose far shrill note the world of new men hears
Cleave the cold shuddering shade as twilight clears;
When song new-born put off the old world's attire
And felt its tune on her changed lips expire,
    Writ foremost on the roll of them that came
Fresh girt for service of the latter lyre,
    Villon, our sad bad glad mad brother's name!

Alas the joy, the sorrow, and the scorn,
    That clothed thy life with hopes and sins and fears,
And gave thee stones for bread and tares for corn
    And plume-plucked gaol-birds for thy starveling peers
    Till death clipt close their flight with shameful shears;
Till shifts came short and loves were hard to hire,
When lilt of song nor twitch of twangling wire
    Could buy thee bread or kisses; when light fame
Spurned like a ball and haled through brake and briar,
    Villon, our sad bad glad mad brother's name!

Poor splendid wings so frayed and spoiled and torn!
    Poor kind wild eyes so dashed with light quick tears!
Poor perfect voice, most blithe when most forlorn,
    That rings athwart the sea whence no man steers
    Like joy-bells crossed with death-bells in our ears!
What far delight has cooled the fierce desire
That like some ravenous bird was strong to tire
    On that frail flesh and soul consumed with flame,
But left more sweet than roses to respire,
    Villon, our sad bad glad mad brother's name?

Envoi

Prince of sweet songs made out of tears and fire,
A harlot was thy nurse, a God thy sire;
    Shame soiled thy song, and song assoiled thy shame.
But from thy feet now death has washed the mire,
Love reads out first at head of all our quire,
    Villon, our sad bad glad mad brother's name.

Algernon Charles Swinburne

Early writers of ballades in English (Dunbar for example), sometimes omitted the envoy and increased the number of verses. There are also double-ballades in both forms; these simply double the number of stanzas preceding the envoy, but stick to the same rhyme scheme.

PANTOUM

A poem of indeterminate length composed of quatrains rhyming abab. The second and fourth line of each quatrain form the first and third lines respectively of the one following. The last stanza alters this slightly by making the second and fourth lines of the penultimate stanza not the first and third of the last stanza, but the third and first respectively. There are few pantoums in English. An amusing one is that quoted by Babette Deutsch in her *Poetry Handbook*, though the final stanza does not follow the formula exactly.

Monologue d'outre Tomb

Morn and noon and night
   Here I lie in the ground;
No faintest glimmer of light,
   No lightest whisper of sound.

Here I lie in the ground;
   The worms glide out and in;
No lightest whisper of sound,
   After a lifelong din.

The worms glide out and in;
   They are fruitful and multiply;
After a lifelong din
   I watch them quietly.

They are fruitful and multiply,
   My body dwindles the while;
I watch them quietly;
   I can scarce forbear a smile.

My body dwindles the while,
   I shall soon be a skeleton;
I can scarce forbear a smile,
   They have had such glorious fun.

I shall soon be a skeleton,
   The worms are wriggling away;
They have had such glorious fun,
   They will fertilize my clay.

The worms are wriggling away,
   They are what I have been;
They will fertilize my clay;
   The grass will grow more green.

They are what I have been.
   I shall change, but what of that?
The grass will grow more green,
   The parson's sheep grow fat.

I shall change, but what of that?
   All flesh is grass, one says.
The parson's sheep grow fat,
   The parson grows in grace.

All flesh is grass, one says;
   Grass becomes flesh, one knows.
The parson grows in grace:
   I am the grace he grows.

Grass becomes flesh, one knows.
   He grows like the bull of Bashan.
I am the grace he grows;
   I startle his congregation.

He grows like the bull of Bashan,
   One day he'll be Bishop or Dean.
I startle his congregation;
   One day I shall preach to the Queen.

One day he'll be Bishop or Dean,
   One of those science-haters;
One day I shall preach to the Queen.
   To think of my going in gaiters!

One of those science-haters,
   Blind as a mole or bat;
To think of my going in gaiters,
   And wearing a shovel hat!

Blind as a mole or bat,
   No faintest glimmer of light,
And wearing a shovel hat,
   Morning and noon and night.

HAIKU

This is a Japanese form. It consists of three lines of five, seven, and five syllables respectively, and does not rhyme or have any metrical regularity. It is supposed to create a pictorial image in such a way as to suggest a particular emotion or a special spiritual insight. Many contemporary American poets have written versions of Haiku, sometimes using the exact syllable-count, and sometimes (especially when translating them from the Japanese) only imitating the tenor and spirit of the form.

> The falling flower
> I saw drift back to the branch
> Was a butterfly.
>
> *Moritake*, translated by Babette Deutsch

TANKA

This is another Japanese form. It consists of five lines. The first and third lines have five syllables each and the others seven. This, like the Haiku, has been much imitated by contemporary American poets.

> Since he is too young
> To know the way, I would plead:
> 'Pray, accept this gift,
> O Underworld messenger,
> And bear the child pick-a-back.'
>
> *Okura*, translated by Babette Deutch

LIMERICK

A familiar form of five lines rhyming aabba, in which the third and fourth lines are shorter than the others and, most frequently, precisely half-size. The form usually demands a quickly moving rhythm, but there is no set metre.

CLERIHEW

This is a four-line poem rhyming aabb, which is supposed to begin with the name of a person to be discussed. It was invented by Edmund Clerihew Bentley. There are no rules other than that the lines must be of unequal length and the result is supposed to be risible.

> Cecil B. de Mille,
> Rather against his will,
> Was persuaded to leave Moses
> Out of 'The Wars of the Roses'.
>
> Nicolas Bentley

By no means all poets are interested in handling these forms, except, perhaps, for amusement. Most young poets find them intolerably difficult. The only way to learn a particular form is to write within it steadily for a week or two, attempting a new poem each day. At the end of this period one finds that one's thoughts naturally fall into the required rhythms, and, what is more, into appropriate patterns of imagery and argument. The learning of a form can thus provide one with a new perspective upon one's perceptions and can cause one to reorder them in novel ways. This often leads to some reworking or development of the set formulae, and to many imaginative discoveries.